THE MEDALLIC PORTRAITS OF SIR WINSTON CHURCHILL

The Medallic Portraits
of Sir Winston Churchill

J. Eric Engstrom

With a Foreword by
The Most Honourable the Marquess of Bath

By appointment
to Her Majesty The Queen
Medallists

By appointment
to H.R.H. The Duke of Edinburgh
Medallists

SPINK & SON LTD
5-7 King Street St. James's
London SW1

737. 209410 904 ENG.

Printed in England by
Robert Stockwell Ltd
London SE1 1YP

Contents

.

Foreword   6

The Medallic Portraits: A Historical Introduction   7

The Catalogue

PART I   Medals and Plaques   13

PART II   Coins   47

Index of Artists   49

Estimated Valuations   50

Churchilliana: A Foreword

By The Most Honourable the Marquess of Bath

It all began over twenty years ago, when I started—in a sort of funny way—collecting Coronation China. In those days crowns were repeatedly being upset and displaced by various rebellions and uprisings, and I thought that Royalty long since had reached their peak in the world, and soon would be no more. That was well over twenty years ago, and I shan't say whether I have changed my opinion!

My collecting interests looked for another object. I asked myself, who would become a man of lasting fame in years to come? Suddenly I realized that Winston Churchill was the obvious answer! His future greatness, despite past successes, was perhaps then obscured by politics of the day and short-sighted contemporaries. I started off by collecting his books only, but the mania grew, and with the years I went on to collect everything to do with him. The result is one of the most comprehensive collections of Churchilliana in England—perhaps in the world—and considering the many fine collections this is no small boast! I won't say it is the rarest or the most valuable because of all the wonderful personal mementos at Chartwell, but it is the most comprehensive in ephemera, all the varied forms of popular tributes to the man. It includes one of the most complete collections of Churchill medals and stamps, not to mention the Sir Edward Marsh collection of letters, the first editions, and Churchill paintings.

The medals are of particular interest for they record Churchill's career in the first war and the second, through political defeat, and then retirement after another period as Prime Minister, and his later birthdays. There are also many memorial pieces and medals for World War II anniversaries. The following catalogue presents these medals in full historical and numismatic detail. The author's labours have been most fruitful!

To my mind there is only one true sign of greatness, and that is someone who can inspire. To me, Sir Winston was not only the greatest Englishman of our time, but the greatest Englishman of all time. I know it will be argued, what of our artists, musicians and poets? What about Shakespeare or our great statesmen and law givers of the past? These men were certainly very great, but they only inspired, I am afraid to say, a minority, whereas Winston Churchill inspired a nation. He inspired a nation to believe that after a fiasco like Dunkirk we were not beaten, and he held this country alone against the might of the German army, with no other country supporting us, and he convinced the British people that we were going to win the war, and we did. Now that is true greatness and this quality was possessed by Sir Winston in abundance.

People who see my collection at Longleat may think it odd that present among the Churchilliana are two pictures done by that other man—Hitler—and may wonder why they are present. One of my reasons for collecting these paintings was my opinion that Churchill would never have been as great a man as he was, had it not been for the challenge presented by Hitler. He had always been anti-Hitler, and when the war came, the British public realized that he was the only man who could effectively tackle such an adversary. It takes opposites to symbolize values in conflict; that is why Hitler is included in my tribute to Churchill.

My only regret is that I never knew Sir Winston really well. I used to meet him in the House of Commons in the pre-war days, and I can remember one little instance there, when a very reputable member of the House came up to me and said: "isn't it a pity, Henry, how finished he is; just a laughing stock, and no-one will ever pay any attention to him again?". I replied: "but surely, whenever he makes a speech"—which in those days was always against Mr. Baldwin—"he fills the House to capacity?" "Ah," said the man, "he fills the House because everyone comes to laugh at him, because he is a very funny speaker, but nobody pays any attention to what he says." By an odd quirk of fate, the man who passed those remarks later became one of Churchill's foremost Ministers in the War Cabinet. We were yet to fully appreciate the extraordinary Churchill!

I have tried in my own way to memorialize the great man. I hope that numismatists may be encouraged by this fine catalogue to honour Sir Winston by possessing one—or a collection—of these enduring tributes in metal.

The Medallic Portraits: A Historical Introduction

The medals commemorating the life and times of Sir Winston Churchill span a period of more than half a century. Yet they do not do justice to his ninety-one years, his influence on modern history, and his extraordinary achievements in this age of specialists and technicians. He was truly a man of many parts: one of the greatest statesmen of the century, Nobel prize-winner, eminent historian of the English-speaking peoples, chronicler of his own times and leadership, academy painter and—above all—the embodiment of the courage and spirit of the British nation.

The words Churchill himself used to describe his illustrious ancestor Marlborough apply to their author with equal force:

> "He was not only the foremost of English soldiers, but in the first rank among the statesmen of our own history; not only that he was a Titan, for that is not disputed, but, that he was a virtuous and benevolent being, eminently serviceable to his age and country, capable of drawing harmony and design from chaos, and one who only needed an earlier and still wider authority to have made a more ordered and a more tolerant civilization for his own time and to help the future."[1]

The medallic record is long; it highlights some of the events of this unique life, and in so doing captures much of modern history. The first Churchill medal, most unfortunately, remained only a design in the sketch book of its artist, the German medallist Karl Goetz. The drawings show an obverse portraying the young Churchill as First Lord of the Admiralty, a position he assumed in 1911 and held until 1915. The proposed legend was: WINSTON (retrograd "s") DER FLOTTENSTRATEGE (Winston, The Fleet Strategist) but careful inspection will show that the

---

[1] Churchill, *Marlborough, His Life and Times* (1933) By permission of the publishers, G. Harrap & Co. Ltd., London.

artist originally had pencilled only WINSTON CHURCHILL. Behind Churchill's neck appears a spurred military boot—no doubt part of some unfinished satire planned by Goetz. The reverse design would seem to depict a maneless British lion, the head shown Hydra-like in different contortions, in terror of the surrounding water, with an exergue date of 1914. This type refers, no doubt, to the beginning of the war and the strengthened German fleet and U-boat packs which would plague the sea lanes. Had this medal been executed it would have been both the first Churchill portrait medal and the only piece showing its subject as a young man.

While it was the purpose of this catalogue to record portrait medals, of necessity several highly important non-portrait pieces mentioning Churchill have been included. Such is the first medal referring to Churchill, a non-portrait, cast by the German, W. Eberbach (catalogue entry 1). Issued either in 1915 or 1916, the medal both satirizes Churchill's resignation as First Lord following the failure of the Gallipoli campaign at the Dardanelles for which he undeservedly received the brunt of the blame until an investigation, and commemorates the successes of the German U-boats against Churchill's fleet and merchant marine. Both events were causes of much rejoicing in Germany, for it had been Churchill who had seen that the British navy was prepared for the war. It is fitting that this satirical first medal records what the Germans, and many Englishmen, saw as the end of Churchill's career, when in fact it was only a preliminary stage of a long public life in which the "finest hour" would come twenty-five years later in a new more terrible war with Germany. The medal stands as an example of ironical under-estimation.

A further medal, again satirical, by Goetz is the second listing in the catalogue. As the entry more fully describes, there is some

Sketch for a Churchill satirical medal by Karl Goetz, 1914 (Kienast Collection)

doubt as to whether Churchill is the figure so identified by the artist at a later date. This medal replies to First Lord of the Admiralty Balfour's Guildhall address of November, 1916, and to the dissemination of a British pamphlet in Sweden, both events referring to Goetz's infamous *Lusitania* medal. The figure identified as Churchill is shown haranguing the medallist.

No British or allied medals record Churchill's role in the First World War either as First Lord, or as a Lieutenant-Colonel in France in 1916, or as a cabinet member during the last war years. Indeed, there are no medals on his very active life in the 1920's nor recording his lone voice crying warnings in the political wilderness of the 1930's.

The first medals of the new war appeared, again, in Germany where Churchill was still respected and feared. The three German medals were modelled by Guido Goetz, Karl's son, as a series of satirical pieces on the early actions at sea and Churchill's return to office. The first is metallic propaganda following exactly the absurd Nazi press releases which blamed the sinking of the passenger liner *Athenia* in the early hours of the war on Churchill personally. The sinking, purported the Nazis, had been arranged as part of a British scheme to draw America into the war by blaming Germany for the subsequent loss of American lives (3). This medal is the first work undisputedly to portray Churchill, and is the only medal to use the full figure besides the questionable attribution of the figure on the Karl Goetz medal from the first war. Following the *Athenia* piece was Guido Goetz's medal on Churchill and the sinking of the aircraft carrier H.M.S. *Courageous* which went down with the captain and much of the crew as the first major Royal Navy loss of the war. This medal, while not portraying Churchill, is directed to him and his name appears in the reverse legend (4). The trio of medals is completed by that issued on German reports of the sinking of the great carrier, the H.M.S. *Ark Royal*, which proved quite false much to bitter German disappointment and subsequent heavy losses. The obverse of this medal portrays Churchill smoking a cigar, and in conference with Prime Minister Neville Chamberlain and Secretary of State for War Leslie Hore-Belisha (5).

All three of the Goetz satiric attacks refer to Churchill as First Lord of the Admiralty, a position he re-assumed after an absence of twenty-four years on September 3, 1939. The works also make use of the death skeleton motif which Eberbach constantly employed on most of his First World War medals, especially in the macabre "Totentanz" or "Dance of Death" medal series of 1916. Guido Goetz's medals were cast during the first flush of German success and enthusiasm for the war in September and November, 1939. They were followed by no others referring to Churchill.

The medallic record now shifts abruptly to England, and Churchill as the new Prime Minister. He had assumed the task of forming a coalition government in May, 1940, and was immediately faced with the dark and bloody months which saw the Dunkirk evacuation, losses at sea, and the opening of the Battle of Britain. It was in these early, troubled months as Prime Minister that at last a British Churchill medallic piece appears. The honour for the first British portrait piece goes to the well-known sculptor Fred I. Kormis who modelled a strong, characteristic likeness of his subject in a large cast plaque (6). The work had been commissioned to illustrate Philip Guedalla's *Mr. Churchill; An Intimate Portrait* which appeared late in 1941. The artist had appointments for sittings with Churchill, but these were cancelled at the last moment because of the Prime Minister's meeting with President Franklin D. Roosevelt at sea in August which saw the formulation of the Atlantic Charter. Mr. Kormis was forced to rely on glimpses of Churchill gained from attending House of Commons addresses earlier, and from photographs. Spink and Son, Ltd. acquired the rights for a limited edition of casts of the plaque. One of the Kormis plaques was presented to Churchill by his Chief of Staff, General Ismay, and he was quite pleased with the work.

The year 1941 also saw a medal by Miss Caroline Magrath who executed the dies on a fine work to commemorate the Atlantic Charter with facing portraits of Churchill and Roosevelt on the reverse, and H.M. King George VI and H.M. Queen Elizabeth on the obverse. Because of restrictions on metals the medal was not struck until after the war (7). The piece was re-issued in 1965 for the twenty-fifth anniversary of the charter using the original reverse as the new obverse with a wreath for the reverse (51).

Mr. F. J. Halnon was responsible for a portrait bust medal of the Prime Minister with his ever-present cigar (8). This piece was cast in lead recovered from the ruins of the House of Commons after the German air raids of May 10, 1941 and was set in small stone blocks from the walls of Parliament. These souvenirs of the Battle of Britain were sold for the benefit of the British Red Cross and St. John Fund in 1942, and number in the thousands.

The war years 1943 and 1944 saw no medals; the lacuna was finally filled by a medal designed by Pierre Turin and issued by the French Mint, Paris, early in 1945. The medal honoured Churchill as a participant in the great Armistice Day parade in liberated Paris on November 11, 1944, and ally in the liberation of the French Empire (11). The piece reproduced part of the Prime Minister's Mansion House speech: "The End of the Beginning" of November 10, 1942. It was the first to use as the reverse design the Churchill family arms, and was the first to show Churchill in military dress.

In this period an undated Canadian commemorative medal by S. Hayman was issued. One of the medals was presented to President Roosevelt before his death in 1945 and is the illustrated example (9).

Probably late in 1944, sometime after his release from a Nazi detention camp, the medallist Theodore Spicer-Simson, while still living at Bourron in occupied France, completed the model of a Churchill portrait medal which is a typically fine piece by this modern master of the art (10). A casting was made of the medal for Churchill after the war, and Spicer-Simson described in his autobiography the circumstances which caused him to create the work:

"While the war was still on an English magazine was passed on to me and in it was a photo of Churchill. He was wearing a thick great-coat but the head in profile was clear, so I saw my opportunity to make a portrait medallion from it, although I dislike doing portraits except from nature. My admiration for him and his wonderful broadcasts that kept up our courage carried the day, so I made one."[2]

The Allied victory and Churchill's leadership were commemorated in a powerfully moving portrait medal by Professor A. Loewental who had been a German medallist in World War I, but who had come to Britain to escape the Nazis. This work made use of the "V for Victory" sign—as had the Hayman medal—as symbolic of the Allied effort and the Prime Minister himself. The tribute reads: UNFLINCHING, INDOMITABLE, HIS SPIRIT SAVED BRITAIN AND SO THE WORLD (12). Originally appearing in 1945, this excellent medal was re-issued in 1965 by B. A. Seaby, Ltd. as a memorial, with the addition of the death date on the portrait truncation and in a reduced size (35).

The coalition government came to an end when Churchill and the Conservatives went down to defeat in the General Elections of 1945. The government which had seen England and the Commonwealth through the war was turned out, and Churchill was embittered, but as a gesture to mark the harmony and accomplishments of the coalition he had struck to his order a special bronze commemorative medal, the design and sentiments being his own. Ordered from Spink & Son, Ltd. in December, 1945, the medals were delivered in August, 1946 and personally distributed by the former Prime Minister to some one-hundred thirty-three senior members of the war-time government and staffs. Each recipient's name was engraved on the reverse, with the legend: TO . . . FROM WINSTON CHURCHILL. The obverse said simply: SALUTE THE GREAT COALITION 1940-1945 (13). A unique silver medal was prepared for presentation to H.M. King George VI. The obverse was that of the bronze medals, but the reverse read: TO THE KING FROM HIS FAITHFUL AND DEVOTED SERVANT WINSTON S. CHURCHILL (14). The medal was presented to the King by Churchill in November, 1946.

---

[2] Spicer-Simson, *A Collector of Characters: Reminiscences of Theodore Spicer-Simson* (1961) By permission of the publishers, University of Miami Press, Coral Gables, Florida.

Four years passed from the Loewental medal until another portrait appeared. Finally in 1949 Frank Kovacs created a uniface cast plaque which is an important Churchill portrait (15). A small re-issue of the plaque was made in 1965. This piece is the only Churchill profile of the several portraits by this artist. It was four more years until the next work was modelled.

Churchill Medal by C. Affer (16)

This was the superb cast medal of 1953 by Costantino Affer of Milan, first shown at the exhibition of European medals sponsored by the Royal Society of Arts in June of 1955 (16). Featuring an exceptional facing portrait which nearly fills the flan, but being slightly off-set by the legend, this *tour de force* remarkably demonstrates "the violent intimacy of the facing portrait", an insight suggested by Dr. C. H. V. Sutherland in his paper on the modern medal for the exhibition. The medal was selected for special praise in an article on Affer's work by Velia Johnson. These comments are included in the catalogue entry.

The following year's offering was a small medal issued in 1954 to commemorate Churchill's eightieth birthday (17). In 1955 the medal was re-issued with a new reverse to honour Churchill's retirement as Prime Minister (18). He had returned as Prime Minister for a second time in 1951, and had become a Knight of the Garter in 1953. In the same year he received the Nobel Prize for literature.

Except for a stray piece first appearing in 1957, but subsequently re-issued in a number of countries as part of a series on the leaders of the Second World War (19), the next Churchill portrait is by Frank Kovacs. The medal was commissioned by Lord Beaverbrook from Spink & Son, Ltd. in commemoration of the "1940 Club" organized by him for friends connected with his service as Minister of Aircraft Production early in the war. Churchill appointed Beaverbrook to the position, and the medal portrays him as "Master Member" of the club (20). The medals were presented to honour the club and Churchill's eighty-fifth birthday in 1959. In that year, another Churchill medal in a "war leaders" series appeared (21).

A grouping of four medals came in 1964 in celebration of Sir Winston's ninetieth birthday and were the work of Schmidt of Austria, Vis of the Netherlands, Ironside of the United Kingdom, and Cademartori of Venezuela (22-25). No medals, unfortunately, were struck in Britain for the occasion.

Artist's model of the Churchill Medal by Rolf Beck (65)

It was with Churchill's death that belated portrait medals began to be issued in recognition of the great man and his many contributions to peace and freedom. In an age in which the medal as an art form and historical document has lost much of its former popularity, it is no small tribute of genuine affection that so many medallic portraits have appeared all over the world. These pieces have been produced in the United States, Canada, Italy, South Africa, Australia, the Netherlands, France, Venezuela, Germany, Switzerland and Austria as well as in the United Kingdom. In addition to the medals and plaques two portraits have appeared on the coinages of the United Kingdom and the Royalist Government of Yemen. Many Churchill memorials have appeared as non-numismatic jewellery pendants and non-metallic plaques.

Some of these recent medals deserve special mention. First it should be noted that in the catalogue medals giving birth and death dates generally have been listed in the entry headings as memorials, while those not specially issued at Churchill's passing, or those connected with particular events of the Second World War have been designated as commemoratives.

The first memorial medal struck would seem to be the medal by Andrew Andrechuk of Canada which first appeared on January 27, 1965, three days after Churchill's death (26). The first British Churchill memorial medals were issued by the artist S. G. M. Adams of Leeds. His first medal appeared one week after Churchill's death (27). It was soon followed by two more productions, all of which were hand-engraved into the dies and produced in limited numbers (28, 41). Several other Churchill portraits and mulings by this artist have appeared (81-84). Adams has done a total of seven Churchill portrait dies.

The Kovacs medal for Spink & Son, Ltd. had been prepared in models before Churchill's death, and the artist had followed his own portrait medal of Churchill done in 1959 for Lord Beaverbrook. Several changes were made; the bust was enlarged and a most original and engaging background of books and paint brushes was added, wonderfully symbolic of Churchill's accomplishments in literature and fine art (30). This medal received wide press coverage and was immediately popular, and, indeed, sparked many of the issues of other medallists. A last Churchill medal designed by Frank Kovacs was issued later in 1965. It too is a fine portrait, and the whole medal's classic simplicity is most appealing (45).

Harald Salomon of the Royal Danish Mint executed a large cast medal in Churchill's memory which he began in January, 1965. This attractive bold piece shows Sir Winston during World War II in a determined pose of tenacity and strength. The reverse is a careful study of Churchill's hand in the famous sign for victory (32).

Excellent portrait medals have been modelled by Paul Vincze of the United Kingdom in his distinctive style (47) and by the Americans Ralph Menconi (31) and Edward Grove (70). The Menconi medal recalls Churchill's honorary United States' citizenship awarded in 1963 and has a most expressive portrait. The obverse and reverse designs by Grove fit each other admirably—a rather rare accomplishment today. Mr. Grove produced his portrait of Churchill after studying some thirty photographs spanning the years of the subject's maturity, and stated "I endeavoured to create a portrait that would be unlike any already issued, that would be recognizably familiar at first glance, yet with a sensitivity of modelling that would reward a more prolonged study". The striking reverse recreates the nightmare that was Dunkirk. Two boatloads of escaping troops are shown approaching a trawler anchored in the harbour—a common scene between May 26th and June 4th, 1940. Above are planes engaged in aerial combat, while smoke from the burning ships and harbour rises in the background. The lighthouse that marks Dunkirk Harbour appears on the horizon. The artist studied a vast number of photographs in the Imperial War Museum collection before producing his work. The Swiss medallist Fritz Jeanneret created a portrait medal which has the bust surrounded by a roughened field, a technique which gives a pleasantly deceptive sense of high relief (58, 59). Costantino Affer has added three more Churchill medals to his credit, thereby being the second medallist—after Adams—with the largest number of distinctive Churchill portraits (29, 33, 34).

One of the medals has a most life-like bust of Churchill with his hand in the "V for Victory" sign, a pose which has caused difficulty for less skilled artists.

The late Elizabeth Wynwood Hahn of Canada followed an original plaster plaque by her husband Emmanuel Hahn which was made at the time of the Quebec Conference of 1943 to achieve a fine profile (42). An expertly modelled cast plaque by Alessandro Colombo of Italy is a major work and a distinguished portrait with a well-positioned legend (71). The Italian medallist Bruno Galoppi has created a most striking modern plaque. The memorable divided portrait and legend fit beautifully the circular flan, utilizing the shadowing qualities possible with cast bronze. Half of the plaque portrays Churchill's outward calm and serenity; half explores inward to his boundless energy, tensions and complexity of mind. The skilfully employed metal stresses hint at the man's surging drives (44).

The versatile Canadian sculptress-medallist Mrs. Dora de Pédery-Hunt has created two outstanding Churchill portraits. Her cast rectangular plaque shows the solitary figure of a seated Churchill, in hat and great-coat, as seen from the back. It is a magnificently original approach to the subject. It evokes in the viewer a sense of the great grandeur and loneliness of a world statesman (75). The artist's Churchill award medal commissioned by Henry R. Jackman of Toronto presents a facing bust with a penetrating cast of the eyes which captures the determination of the man and his forthrightness in all good causes. This sensitive portrait is particularly appropriate for a medal awarded to students for excellence. A worthy model for further endeavours is presented (80).

The 1969 medal by Gasparro and others of the U.S. Mint is a fine and unusual portrait (86). Instead of the belligerent, defiant war Prime Minister, it shows a "retired" Churchill with the countenance of a visionary with faith in the future for the post-war world but aware of the dangers. Out of office and dressed as an academic, this medal portrays him at the moment he delivered his "Sinews of Peace" speech of March, 1946 at Westminster College, in Missouri. There, hope for the future was matched by an admonishment on the reality of the "Iron Curtain" which had descended dividing Europe.

Churchill Plaque by D. de Pédery-Hunt (75)

The reverse of the medal depicts the London church, reconstructed on the college campus, which is the centre of the Churchill Memorial and Library. Twenty-three years after his speech, this memorial is a testament to continued co-operation between the United Kingdom and the United States. Churchill, at the end of his life, was immensely pleased at the prospect of the project. By act of Congress a special gold striking of this medal was minted for presentation to his widow. The Senate bill read:

"Be it enacted by the Senate and House of Representatives of the United States of America in Congress assembled, That . . . in honor of the dedication of the Winston Churchill Memorial and Library at Westminster College in Fulton, Missouri, in May, 1969, the President is authorized to present in the name of the people of the United States and in the name of the Congress to the widow of the late Winston Churchill a gold medal with suitable emblems, devices, and inscriptions to be determined . . . subject to the approval of the Secretary of the Treasury. The Secretary shall cause such a medal to be struck and furnished to the President.

An important event in Churchillian portraiture and the sequel to an interesting numismatic story came about with the Churchill and the twenty-fifth anniversary of the D-Day Invasion medal by Oscar Nemon sculpted in 1969 (87). The portrait is that of Prime Minister Churchill during the later war years. Looking at this impressive and dynamic portrait with its unusual positioning, one's eyes are immediately drawn to the massive, heavy brow and Churchill's jutting chin, and they then travel across to the broad lettering of the name, positioned to complement these unique features: CHURCHILL. The viewer is struck by the medal subject's brooding intelligence and surging energies as conveyed by deft modelling of the facial features with a roughened texture, which is slightly impressionistic. The artist has expressed in this miniature work his concept of Churchill's spirit which is found in his other Churchills, most especially in his heroic statue in the House of Commons: "the idea of impatience and hurry, of a man wanting to see something done".

The reminder of the D-Day Invasion on the lower obverse recalls that great epic and Churchill's determination to be a physical part of it by crossing with the invasion fleet. When General Eisenhower refused him permission to sail, the Prime Minister replied that he would join the crew of a British vessel over which the Supreme Commander had no immediate control. It was only when H.M. King George VI insisted that if Churchill went, so would he, that the Prime Minister reluctantly gave the plan up. Four days after the beach-head, Churchill visited Normandy, just as later he personally crossed the Rhine soon after Allied troops had established a bridge-head in Germany.

Nemon met Churchill in Marrakesh in 1950 and they became close friends. In fact Churchill's only sculpture was a bust of Nemon which he presented to the artist. It was through this friendship as well as Nemon's eminence as a sculptor that Nemon's design was accepted for the Churchill commemorative Crown of 1965. Nemon's portrait for the piece was derived from the profile of the bust which he did of Churchill in a "siren suit" for H.M. Queen Elizabeth II, which is now at Windsor.

The Churchill Crown was a controversial coin, despite its tremendous mintage, with some critics disliking its low relief and impressionistic treatment of Churchill, and others finding Nemon's reverse inharmonious with Mary Gillick's obverse. Oscar Nemon himself did not consider the model he submitted to the Royal Mint to be fully finished, and he wished additional time to complete it. But due to public pressure for the proposed coin the Royal Mint began the dies and Nemon was unable to add the detailing and rework the relief as he wished.

While the result was an imaginative and unusual coin portrait, the artist was not satisfied. He desired to produce a definitive Churchill medallic portrait which would more fully demonstrate his medallist's talents. This medal gave the artist such an opportunity and the medallic portrait is now Nemon's finished Churchill, the final development of the Churchill Crown portrait.

An interesting set of four medals (88, 89, 90, 91) was designed by David Cornell and issued in England in 1970 to commemorate Churchill and the twenty-fifth anniversary of peace in Europe. The legendless obverses portray an active Churchill:

uniformed, delivering an address, pensive before a radio broadcast, and displaying the victory sign. The four reverses show
inscribed tablets bearing some of Churchill's most famous
quotations.

Other medals are well-deserving of note. They are those by
the distinguished medallist Leslie Pinches (39), Hans Diller (43),
Joseph Hazeldine (54, 68), the two by Geoffrey Colley (50, 74),
Alessandro Colombo and Vincenzo Gasperetti (56), W. A.
Pater and E. J. Kohler (37, 38), Anthony Foley and Kenneth
Hunt (46), the several pieces using the same portrait by Miss
Caroline Magrath (60-63), Rolf Beck (65), Gerald Benny and
Stuart Devlin (66), Michael Rizzello (67), Werner Gutbrod (72),
the unusual bust by Arnold Machin (76), Mrs. Cecile Curtis (78),
A. Tromp and David MacGregor (69), and Geoffrey Hearn (57).

Fortunately most of the medals issued since Sir Winston's
death have been competently done, although there are some
uninspiring exceptions with poorly worked portraits and pedes-
trian reverses. Part of this criticism is the natural result of the
trend towards striking medals in low relief which results in both
a cheaper product in cost terms, but often an inferior portrait.

Lacking, too, has been originality, generally, in reverse types.
In the past commemorative medals have usually shown obverse
and reverse designs which are smoothly intergrated in style and
symbolism. On several of these pieces there is no unity and no
dominant theme. While the "V for Victory" sign and the
Churchill family arms have been overworked, they are at least
appropriate. The Kovacs medal for Spink & Son, Ltd. which
makes use of Sir David Low's famous cartoon was an interesting
choice for the lone soldier on the medal symbolizes both Britain
and Churchill. The Vincze, Menconi and Grove medals have
already been mentioned and have well-executed reverses in
keeping with their obverses. The clock-face and Parliament
reverse of Affer's medal (34) is nicely done, Adams' lion is
properly defiant (41), and a number of other medals show
careful thought.

The author has attempted to mention in the catalogue entries
the principle photographic source for the artist's portrait.
Naturally, most of the medallic portraits are the resulting
composite of many likenesses, but nevertheless, the most
popular guide for artists has been the famous photographic study of a
pugnacious Churchill made by Yousuf Karsh of Canada in
1941. No medals were modelled from life, and most artists
worked from news photographs of the war period or from the
photographic portraits made in 1953, 1954, and 1955. Churchill
was, as his son Randolph wrote, one of the most photographed
and one of the most photogenic men of the century. Artists
have, therefore, been able to work from an almost endless
source of likenesses for their portraits, but all, with the exception
of the disputed Karl Goetz medal, have portrayed their subject
in the era 1939-1955. Several of the medallic portraits are
exceptionally inspired representations. The greatest of them can
compete with the Churchill portraits in oil, bronze and marble
by such distinguished artists as Orpen, Birley, Graham Sutherland, Nemon and Epstein.

Perhaps the future will see further important Churchill
medals issued to commemorate events in his early career, or
continuing to appear as records of the anniversary of Second
World War events. The centennial of Sir Winston's birth which
will occur in 1974 will hopefully be noted by appropriate medals.

The Churchill medals continue a trend of commemoration
and memorialization in metal dating from the Renaissance
which is worthy of preservation and expansion for the benefit
of future historians and numismatists, and which may serve as
continuing inspiration for our own times. The properties of the
commemorative portrait medal create an intimate personal
involvement with the subject. The restrictive confines of the
circular medal form require forceful messages, all excess cut,
and portraits which can capture the viewer from miniature.
With a Titanic figure such as Churchill much understanding and
skill is needed to convey the essence of greatness from such a
small area.

Some of the medals capture this spirit, but most can only
hope to be imperishable tributes of devotion evoking the proud
imperative in Westminster Abbey: "Remember Winston
Churchill".

Churchill Medal by Frank Kovaks (45)

The Catalogue

The listings are as complete as it was possible to compile with due diligence over a five-year period, but for any errors, omissions of medals or fuller details, the author would be indebted to readers bringing such information to his attention.

Each medal has been given a letter designation following the catalogue number in order to accommodate the many metals, sizes and weights in which a particular piece may occur. The order of listing is by metal, descending vertically: platinum, gold (AV), silver gilt (AR gilt), silver (AR), cupro-nickel, goldine, bronze gilt (Æ gilt), bronze (Æ), copper, iron, aluminium, and lead. Horizontally the listings are by metal, millimeter size, metal finenesses per 1,000 (24 kt. is .999 22 kt. is .916, 18 kt. is .750 and 9 kt. is .375. Sterling silver is .920, Britannia silver is .960), weight in grammes for platinum, gold and silver strikings, and the number of medals issued when known. For the last fact it should be noted that in many cases the total allowable issue has not been reached, but may later be struck.

The word "numbered" following a medal listing indicates that each medal of the particular type is individually numbered, serially, on its rim. When no figure or word appears the issue was unlimited and unnumbered. In most instances the medal dies are still extant unless their cancellation has been noted.

Finenesses, weights, and numbers issued are those provided by the medallists or emitting firms. In the entries no mention has been made of hallmarks or other metal stamps, nor reference to the type of casing for the medal or sets as issued. Special sets have been noted of the same medal in different metals or sizes. Such sets generally contain medals with matching serial numbers.

The medals are arranged in chronological order of issuance, by year for the earlier pieces, and by month of production or first publication notice for the latter issues.

Part I catalogues all known medals and plaques, Part II lists coins. The author has refrained, by purpose, from listing non-numismatic Churchill portraits such as jewellery pendants, charms, and non-metallic pieces. These are not collected by numismatists, and have no place here, although they are a part of Churchilliana.

I believe that my method of cataloguing states the essential information which the numismatist desires for medals, and I can only suggest that the medallic art firms—when releasing information about their new medals—should attempt to give these essentials. Much needless correspondence could thus be eliminated and future collectors would be assured of comprehensive details on medal issues.

References are to the following institutional or publicly-displayed collections:

American Numismatic Society, New York City
Ashmolean Museum, University of Oxford, Oxford
Marquess of Bath, Longleat, Warminster, Wilts.
British Museum, London
Chartwell, Westerham, Kent
Fitzwilliam Museum, University of Cambridge, Cambridge
Kadman Numismatic Museum, Museum Haaretz, Tel Aviv
National Maritime Museum, Greenwich
Franklin D. Roosevelt Library, Hyde Park, New York
Smithsonian Institution, Washington
University of Oslo Coin Cabinet, Oslo

Churchill Memorial and Library, Westminster College, Fulton, Missouri

Private collections are as indicated. Many of the Churchill medals in the American Numismatic Society collection were donated by the Honourable R. Henry Norweb, and the Kadman Numismatic Museum medals are part of the Frankenhuis collection.

The author is indebted to the many artists, medallic art houses, collectors and curators who supplied essential information and listed their collections. Space does not permit a fuller acknowledgement of my gratitude to these many persons.

Above all I am deeply thankful for the interest of the Most Honourable, the Marquess of Bath, whose superb medal collection formed the basis for this work and who graciously contributed the foreword.

Mrs. Joan S. Martin of the British Museum was ever-willing to provide information and undertake research. The late Carsten Svarstad of the University of Oslo gave considerable aid, and the late J. D. A. Thompson of the Ashmolean, my former Oxford mentor, offered early advice and encouragement to the project.

I thank Henry Grunthal of the American Numismatic Society for his many kindnesses, and for his magnaminous gesture in sharing material he had accumulated for a similar catalogue. Miss Grace Hamblin, National Trust administrator at Chartwell, co-operated with the attempt at a definitive catalogue. Mr. Gunter W. Kienast supplied much information on the German satirical medals, while Charles Casey undertook needed photographic work. James C. Risk and D. Wayne Johnson also aided my efforts. Lastly, Howard Linecar and E. C. Joslin of Spink & Son gave much editorial help and proved enthusiastic in supplying details of several issues.

Photos of medals number 10 and 12 are by courtesy of the Heberden Coin Room, Ashmolean Museum; medal 9 is by permission of the Franklin D. Roosevelt Library, medal 13 is reproduced by courtesy of the Trustees of the National Maritime Museum. Illustrations of medals 14 and 35 were allowed by the Department of Coins and Medals of the British Museum. The photo of the Churchill crown is the official release by the British Information Services.

PART I *Medals and Plaques*

1 Churchill, First Lord of the Admiralty, Satirical Medal, 1916

By W. EBERBACH, Germany

Emitted by W. Eberbach, Strassburg

Cast by W. Eberbach, Strassburg

A. Iron 83 mm.

Although the date of this medal is unknown, it would seem to date from Churchill's period as First Lord in 1915 or perhaps after the Gallipoli campaign in 1916. A similar reverse was used by the artist for another medal on Balfour as First Lord of the Admiralty which would post-date this medal.

Obverse:

Nude warrior (Siegfried?) in helmet, armed with short sword and shield attacking a huge monster representing British sea power. All within a pellet ring; outside, wave design and legend. Legend: HURRA GERMANIA, BRITANNIA RULE THE WAVES Right Field: WE (monogram)

Reverse:

Inscription and U-boat with German ensign below. All within a pellet ring, outside is a wave design. Legend: SIR (sic) /WINSTON· CHURCHILL / DEM · SEEGEWALTIGEN (Sir Winston Churchill, Ruler of the Seas) Exergue: W. EBERBACH

Collections:

A.N.S., Marquess of Bath, British Museum, National Maritime Museum

2 Lord Balfour and the *Lusitania*, Satirical Medal, 1916

By KARL GOETZ, Germany

Emitted by Karl Goetz, Munich

Cast by Karl Goetz, Munich

A. Æ 58 mm.
B. Æ 58 mm.
C. Iron 58 mm. } 200
D. Æ 50 mm.

The furor concerning Karl Goetz's famous *Lusitania* satirical medal is well known. The medal caused a great deal of comment in the U.S. and in the U.K. and the artist felt he was being unjustly condemned for this medal which he defended as a piece of satire not intended as a gleeful monument to the loss of life as his critics saw it. An account of this medal may be found in Gunter W. Kienast's *The Medals of Karl Goetz* (Artus Co., Cleveland, 1967), at p. 65.

Arthur Balfour followed Churchill as First Lord of the Admiralty in May, 1915, in the Asquith government, and on November 9, 1916, he addressed the Lord Mayor's banquet at Guildhall. Asquith was also present. Balfour explained the military unimportance of the recent Channel Raid, and then launched an attack on German unrestricted submarine warfare as a violation of the Hague Conference of 1909, recalling the German representative's speech at the conference in which he said that the officers of the German navy would always fulfill "in the strictest manner the duties which result from the unwritten laws of humanity and civilization". Balfour then concluded:

"What are we to say of a nation which makes such a speech from the mouth of its chosen representative at an assembly of the nations considering international law at The Hague, and in a few years afterwards strike a medal for the sinking of the *Lusitania?*"

It would seem that these words were reported in Germany and caused Goetz to issue this medallic response to the Balfour speech, coupled with a retort to a British pamphlet circulating in Sweden which had been mentioned in the *Bayerische Staatszeitung* of September 18, 1916. This article is reported by Kienast to have been in Goetz's personal scrapbook and seems to be the source of this medal's reverse. The news article says that the British pamphlet, entitled "A German Naval Victory", "exploits the sinking of the *Lusitania* in a very derogatory manner. The pamphlet shows the picture of a commemorative medal which allegedly was minted in Germany on this occasion". Commenting on British misrepresentation the article continues "this is only topped by the statement that Germany minted a commemorative medal on the occasion of the *Lusitania* sinking. This is an absolute manufactured lie . . ." It therefore appears that knowledge of Goetz's private medal—which was of course, not an official piece—was very limited.

The artist assigned opus number 156A to this medal and in his description of it he identified the obverse figures as Balfour at the lectern showing the *Lusitania* medal to Lords Grey and Asquith, with Churchill in the background assailing the artist Goetz. This identification seems improper in several aspects, and was made some years later by Goetz. The figure facing, holding a magnifying glass, is undoubtedly David Lloyd George, the Secretary of State for War from June to December 1916, and Prime Minister from December of that year. The figure bending over to inspect the medal is Sir Edward Grey who was Foreign Secretary until December, 1916.

The background figure is more difficult. While it could be Churchill, the portrait is not similar to that of Churchill by Goetz drawn as a sketch for a Churchill medal in 1914 which was never produced. Additionally, Churchill had been out of the government since 1915, and had only just returned from the Western Front to re-enter politics at the time this medal was executed. Prime Minister Herbert Asquith would seem a more likely candidate to be suggested by this figure, and it does bear a certain resemblance to him, but in deference to Goetz's own description this medal is included as depicting Churchill.

13

The combination of the Balfour speech obverse and the British *Lusitania* pamphlet in Sweden on the reverse is common to much of Goetz's work which couples two separate events referring to the same subject in one medal.

The total number of medals issued is unknown but thought to be perhaps two hundred. Medal D shows a doubling of part of the reverse legend, and a mold crack on the reverse besides being smaller than the others. It would seem to be a slightly later cast by Goetz.

Obverse:
Full figure of First Lord of the Admiralty Balfour at a lecturn to right, with his extended hand exhibiting Goetz's *Lusitania* medal to the Secretary of State for War, David Lloyd George, facing, viewing through a magnifying glass, and to Foreign Secretary Sir Edward Grey bending to left. In the background former First Lord of the Admiralty Churchill (or Prime Minister Asquith) harangues Karl Goetz who holds a medal sketchbook. Legend: DIFFICILE EST SATIRAM NON SCRIBERE · (It is difficult not to write a satire) Exergue: DIE · LVSITANIA · MVNZE / GIBT · LORD · BALFOUR / STOFF · Z · REDEN / 9·XI·1916 (The *Lusitania* medal gives Lord Balfour speech material, November 9, 1916)

Reverse:
A Scottish bagpiper walking to right, playing his pipes, wearing placards on his front and back inscribed: ENGL(ISCHES) / FLUG / BLATT / EIN / DEUTSCHER / SEE SIEG (An English pamphlet: A German Naval Victory), two faces of a medal inscribed, left: LU / SITA / NI / A, right: M / EDAI / LLE, below: 1916 (*Lusitania* Medal, 1916). Legend: ENGLISCHE · HETZ ARBEIT IN SCHWEDEN English smear propaganda in Sweden)

Collections:
Engstrom, Kienast

clear indication of German unrestricted warfare by submarines, and a resumption of the old terror of the First World War. The charge received wide publicity in Germany as this medal testifies. This piece incorporates all of the propaganda concocted by the Nazis. Churchill, recalling the incident in *The Second World War: The Gathering Storm*, wrote: "The German Government immediately issued a statement that I personally had ordered a bomb to be placed on board this vessel in order by its destruction to prejudice German-American relations. This falsehood received some credence in unfriendly quarters".

Obverse:
Full figure of Churchill seated on a wooden shipping crate inscribed: VORS(SICHT) HÖLLEN / MASCHINE (Caution: Infernal Machine). The attached shipping tag reads: AN MR. / CHURCHILL (To Mr. Churchill). Churchill holds in his left hand a balance scale, a bomb marked with a Union Jack in the far balance, a torpedo with swastika in the near balance which Churchill points out with his right hand, as his left hand tips the scale to weigh down the torpedo. Legend: EIN MEISTER DER LÜGE (A Master of the Lie)

Reverse:
Passenger liner inscribed: ATHENIA on the starboard side of the bow, breaking waves steaming to right. Skeleton figure of death straddles the bow, facing, slightly to right, holding a torch in its right hand, and a bomb with Union Jack in its left hand. Legend: 4 SEPTEMBER 1939 Exergue: GUIDO GOETZ

Collections:
Marquess of Bath, Engstrom, Kienast

3 Churchill and the Sinking of the *Athenia*, Satirical Medal, 1939

By GUIDO GOETZ, Germany

Emitted by Guido Goetz, Munich

Cast by Karl and Guido Goetz, Munich

A.	Æ 70 mm.	20
B.	Iron 70 mm.	100
C.	Porcelain 70 mm.	20

Upon returning as First Lord of the Admiralty on September 3, 1939, Churchill addressed the House of Commons the very next day. His first statement concerned the sinking of the Donaldson Atlantic liner *Athenia* which was sunk a few hours after the declaration of war by the German submarine U-30. The crowded passenger liner was sunk off Ireland with a heavy loss of life, including some Americans. The First Lord commented: "She was torpedoed without the slightest warning in circumstances which the whole opinion of the world after the late war, in which Germany concurred, has stigmatized as inhuman".

Following the sinking the Nazi propagandist Goebbels denied that a German U-boat had attacked the *Athenia*, instead, he charged that there had been an explosion of an "infernal machine" hidden on the liner under Churchill's own orders as part of a nefarious scheme to create a new *Lusitania* incident which would snare the United States into the war immediately— a typical example of perfidious Albion's work according to the Nazis.

The absurdness of the claim was apparent in the United States and the United Kingdom and was seen by the newspapers as a

4 Churchill and the Sinking of H.M.S. *Courageous*, Satirical Medal, 1939

By GUIDO GOETZ, Germany

Emitted by Guido Goetz, Munich

Cast by Guido and Karl Goetz, Munich

A.	Æ 70 mm.	20
B.	Iron 70 mm.	100

The early days of the war at sea saw heavy British losses which were Churchill's duty to report as First Lord. The Royal Navy's first major loss of the Second World War was the aircraft carrier H.M.S. *Courageous*, a ship originally built as a cruiser for the first war, and later converted into a carrier. Churchill announced in the House that the ship had been turning into the wind to receive homing airplanes when the U-boat made its attack. While the carrier had four destroyers as escorts, two were away after another U-boat reported attacking a merchant vessel. It was due to this combination of circumstances that what Churchill called a "hundred-to-one chance" came off, and the U-boat hit its mark causing a loss of over five-hundred men and many aircraft on September 17, 1939, as the ship sank in the Bristol Channel. This medal, issued soon afterwards, is dated wrongly as are all these works which were inspired by often erroneously dated press reports, and hurriedly modelled and cast while the event was still topical.

Obverse:
Neptune rising from the sea, holding on his right shoulder the sunken aircraft carrier *Courageous*. The name of the ship is inscribed on the port side of the bow, aircraft are visible on the flight deck. In his left hand Neptune holds a trident, a small Union Jack hangs at his left side. Legend: RULE BRITANNIA! Right Field: GUIDO GOETZ

Reverse:
Cloaked skeleton figure of death emerges from the sea to right, holding in its left hand a paper headed by a large incuse swastika, inscribed incuse: TORPED. / VON / DEUTSCH. / "U" / BOOT / 18. SEPT. 1939 (Torpedoed by a German U-boat, September 18, 1939)   Legend: DIE HIOBSBOTSCHAFT AN CHURCHILL (Job's message of bad news to Churchill)

Collections:
Engstrom, Kienast

5   The H.M.S. *Ark Royal*, Satirical Medal, 1939

By GUIDO GOETZ, Germany

Emitted by Guido Goetz, Munich

Cast by Guido and Karl Goetz, Munich
A.   Æ 70 mm.   20
B.   Iron 70 mm.   100

One-hundred-fifty miles off the Norwegian coast a British naval squadron which included the aircraft carrier H.M.S. *Ark Royal*, was attacked by a flight of twenty German bombers in the first action in history between men-of-war at sea and a large airplane bombing force. The battle of September 26, 1939, was portentous for the war. Although no Royal Navy losses resulted from the engagement, the Nazis claimed that the *Ark Royal* had been sunk and a battleship badly damaged. The Germans continued to claim the carrier's destruction. Prime Minister Neville Chamberlain commented on October 3rd that the *Ark Royal* was continuing to perform its duties "sublimely unconscious of rumours that she had been sunk". Writing in *The Second World War: The Gathering Storm*, Churchill recalled the event:

> "The Germans claimed she had been sunk and the pilot who made the claim was decorated. For weeks afterwards the German wireless reiterated daily the question: 'Where is the *Ark Royal*' ".

The First Lord addressed the House in a report on the war at sea recalling the losses of H.M.S. *Courageous*, *Royal Oak* and *Oxley* on November 8th. In the course of the address he sounded a lighter note:

> "It is interesting to note that one of the most valuable of recent prizes was captured from the enemy by the *Ark Royal*, which the German wireless has sunk so many times. When I recall the absurd claims which they are accustomed to shout around the world, I cannot resist saying we should be quite content to engage the entire German Navy, using only the vessels which at one time or another they have declared they have destroyed".

The famous carrier was torpedoed near Gibraltar by a U-boat on November 13, 1941, and sank causing only one casualty. It was the end of a distinguished career and a serious blow to the navy, but not as serious as its loss would have been in 1939, which explains the long German propaganda barrage suggesting its sinking, reported by this medal, which sought to undermine the British people's faith in the government's reports on the war—thus the obverse legend. The medal has an erroneous date.

Obverse:
A pensive Prime Minister Chamberlain seated at table, half-figure facing, flanked on the left by First Lord of the Admiralty Churchill smoking a cigar, half-figure to right. Chamberlain is flanked on the right by Secretary of State for War Leslie Hore-Belisha, hand to face, half-figure to left. Churchill's extended right hand supports paper inscribed incuse: DEUTSCHE / BOMBER / GEGEN / BRIT. SEE- / STREITKRÄFTE / 27. SEPT. 39 (German

bombers against British naval forces, September 27, 1939). The table before the seated figures shows incuse: CH., below Churchill, and LHB (around a Star of David) below Hore-Belisha who is incongruously shown in a military uniform! Legend: WIE SAG ICHS MEINEN VOLKE (How do I tell my people?)

Reverse:
German bomber showing incuse swastika and crosses to right above a skeleton figure of death, with skull looking upward to right, holding a Union Jack in the waves of an explosion-filled sea. Flag inscribed: ARK / ROYAL / ?   Left Field: GUIDO GOETZ (incuse)

Collections:
Marquess of Bath, Engstrom, Kienast

6   Churchill, Prime Minister, Commemorative Plaque, 1941

By FRED I. KORMIS, United Kingdom

Emitted by Spink & Son, Ltd., London

Cast by the Morris Singer Foundry Ltd., London
A.   Æ 127 mm.   50 uniface casts

This extremely fine, high-relief piece was the first exceptional Churchill portrait medal. The work was commissioned by Hodder & Stoughton Ltd., publishers, to serve as illustration for Philip Guedalla's *Mr. Churchill: An Intimate Portrait*, which was published late in 1941. The author had arranged for the artist to have Churchill sit for the work, but this arrangement was cancelled at the very last moment because of Churchill's departure for his meeting with Roosevelt which resulted in the Atlantic Charter.

Faced by the printing deadline, the artist was forced to rely on his memory of Churchill gained from observing him in the House of Commons and from photographs. The result was an imaginative, and forceful interpretation. General Ismay presented Churchill with one of the casts and he was quite pleased with the likeness.

Spink & Son secured the rights for a limited issue of the piece. Most of the fifty casts carry the artist's signature etched on the reverse.

Obverse:
Bust of Churchill to left. Legend: WINSTON CHURCHILL 1941 Right Field: KORMIS (incuse)

Reverse:
Uniface

Collections:
Marquess of Bath, Chartwell, Churchill Memorial and Library, Engstrom

7   Atlantic Charter Commemorative Medal, 1941

By CAROLINE MAGRATH, United Kingdom

Emitted by Turner & Simpson, Ltd., Birmingham

Struck by Turner & Simpson, Ltd., Birmingham
A.   Æ 76 mm.   .925   210 grms.   4

This interesting piece was designed, and the dies were cut, in 1941 to commemorate the signing of the Atlantic Charter in August, 1941, concluded by Churchill and Roosevelt. The charter was to prove of great importance for the war and in the founding of the United Nations. The emitting firm was unable to strike medals owing to the Restriction of Supply Order of

1941. In 1948 four strikings were made, and one was presented to Mrs. Roosevelt, and one to Churchill. The Churchill portrait became the model for the artist's 1965 Churchill memorial medals. In 1965 for the 25th anniversary of the Atlantic Charter, gold strikings of the reverse only of this medal were made, the reverse being used as an obverse with the addition of a wreath reverse type.

Obverse:
In inner circle, crowned busts of King George VI and Queen Elizabeth, conjoined, to right. Legend: GEORGE VI   QUEEN ELIZABETH

Reverse:
Profile portraits of Franklin D. Roosevelt and Winston S. Churchill in half-circle medallions, facing, with crossed American and British flags, with olive branch between, connected by a riband with date 1941. Legends under each bust and in central exergue. Legend: TO / COMMEMORATE / THE ATLANTIC CHARTER
Left Field: ROOSEVELT   Right Field: CHURCHILL

Collections:
Marquess of Bath, Chartwell, Roosevelt Library

9   Churchill Commemorative Medal, 1945

By S. HAYMAN, Canada

Emitter and striker unknown
A.   Æ 64 mm.

This medal is known to the author only from the piece presented to President Franklin D. Roosevelt, and dates before his death in 1945. Exact date or reason for issue are not known, although the piece would appear to have been issued for a visit by Churchill to Canada, probably in 1944 or 1945.

Obverse:
Bust of Churchill to left, in great-coat. Legend: RT. HON. WINSTON CHURCHILL   Truncation: S. HAYMAN (incuse)

Obverse:
Large "V for Victory" sign, lighted torch and Canadian arms shield superimposed. Legend: CANADA COME, THEN, LET US TO OUR TASK

Collections:
Franklin D. Roosevelt Library

8   Churchill and the Battle of Britain Commemorative Medal, 1942

By F. J. HALNON, United Kingdom

Emitted by the British Red Cross and St. John Fund, London

Cast by London Stonecraft Ltd., London
A.   Lead 70 mm. (attached to stone 125 mm. × 100 mm.)

This most interesting piece was issued in several thousand examples with the following certificate signed and numbered:

> FROM SIR VINCENT BADDELEY, K.C.B. to whom the material recovered from the damaged House of Commons following the air-raid on London in 1941 has been supplied by H.M. Ministry of Works and Buildings to be disposed of for certain charitable purposes.   LONDON, E.C., England
>
> VB/BSB   13th May, 1942
>
> I hereby certify that this stone was part of the structure of the Houses of Parliament, damaged by enemy air raids on 10th May, 1941.
>
> (signed) Vincent Baddeley

Obverse:
Bust of Churchill with cigar, facing, to left,. Legend: WINSTON CHURCHILL 1941

Reverse:
Uniface

Collections:
Marquess of Bath

10   Churchill Commemorative Medal, 1945

By THEODORE SPICER-SIMSON, United States.

Emitted by Theodore Spicer-Simson, Miami

Cast by the Medallic Art Company, New York
A.   Æ 85 mm.   1 uniface cast
B.   Æ 85 mm.   6 uniface galvano casts

The quotation from the artist's autobiography concerning this medal may be found in the introduction. The artist modelled the medal while living in Bourron, in occupied France towards the end of World War II. While Spicer-Simson worked almost entirely from life for his superb medallic portraits, necessity forced him to use a magazine photograph for this distinctive Churchill portrait. Cast after the war, the original casting was presented to Churchill. At various times additional specimens were authorized by the artist or his widow.

Obverse:
Bust of Churchill to left in great-coat. Legend: WINSTON CHURCHILL Left Field: TSS (monogram) / 1945

Reverse:
Uniface

Collections:
Ashmolean, Marquess of Bath, British Museum, Chartwell, Engstrom, Mrs. T. Spicer-Simson, University of Miami Library

11 Churchill and the Liberation of France Commemorative Medal, 1945

By PIERRE TURIN, France

Emitted by the French Mint, Paris

Struck by the French Mint, Paris
A. A̅′ 68 mm. .920
B. A̅′ 68 mm. .750
C. Æ̅ 68 mm. .950
D. Æ 68 mm.

This medal has been available from the French Mint since 1945 when it was issued to honor the liberation, and Churchill's visit to Paris for the Armistice Day Parade of November 11, 1944. Since 1966 strikings of the medal have carried the year made on the rims in addition to indications of metal and fineness. This medal and the Loewental piece are important as the two "victory" medals portraying Churchill which were generally available at the end of World War II.

Obverse:
Bust of Churchill in uniform, slightly to left, after a photograph taken in Germany during his inspection tour of March, 1945. Legend: WINSTON CHURCHILL Left Field: PIERRE TURIN / MCMVL

Reverse:
Churchill family arms and inscription below. The arms show a shield quartering the arms of Churchill with those of Spencer. The dexter crest is of Churchill and the sinister is of Spencer, with the scroll motto: FIEL PERO DESDICHADO (Faithful Though Unfortunate). The inscription is a quotation in French from "The End of the Beginning" speech at the Lord Mayor's Day luncheon, Mansion House, on November 10, 1942. Legend: NOUS N'AVONS QU'UN DÉSIR / VOIR UNE FRANCE FORTE ET LIBRE / ENTOURÉE DE SON EMPIRE ET RÉUNIE A L'ALSACE-LORRAINE / 10 NOVEMBRE 1942 (For ourselves we have no wish but to see France free and strong, with her Empire gathered round her and with Alsace-Lorraine restored).

Collections:
A.N.S., Marquess of Bath, Engstrom, Kadman, Oslo

12 Churchill and the Allied Victory Commemorative Medal, 1945

By A. LOEWENTAL, United Kingdom

Emitted by Harry Burrows, Jeweller, Manchester

Struck by John Pinches (Medallists) Ltd., London
A. Æ 63 mm. 1000

Obverse:
Bust of Churchill to left. Legend: CHURCHILL Left Field: 1945 (Victory sign incuse, date superimposed) Truncation: A. LOEWENTAL / LINCOLN

Reverse:
Hand, rising from cloud, holding victory torch. Legend: · UNFLINCHING · INDOMITABLE · HIS · SPIRIT · SAVED · BRITAIN · AND · SO · THE · WORLD · Left and Right Fields: WE · WILL FIGHT · ON / LAND ON · SEA / AND · IN THE · AIR / UNTIL VICTORY IS WON · Exergue: AL (incuse monogram)

Collections:
Chartwell, Engstrom, Fitzwilliam, Oslo, Franklin D. Roosevelt Library

13 Churchill War Coalition Cabinet Presentation Medal, 1946

By WINSTON S. CHURCHILL, United Kingdom

Emitted by Winston S. Churchill, London

Struck by Spink & Son, Ltd., London
A. Æ 112 mm. 133 (engraved to recipient)

This medal was prepared at Churchill's instruction for presentation to senior members of the wartime coalition government and members of the armed services following the end of the coalition government in the General Elections of 1945. The medal was ordered in December, 1945, and delivered in August, 1946 for distribution by the former Prime Minister.

The following individuals received the engraved medals, the names were in the following order: *Clement Attlee, Anthony Eden, John Anderson, Ernest Bevin, Oliver Lyttelton, Herbert Morrison, Woolton, Halifax, Simon, Cranborne, Beaverbrook, Leo Amery, Oliver Stanley, Albert Victor Alexander, P. J. Grigg, Archibald Sinclair, Tom Johnston, Andrew Duncan, Stafford Cripps, Swinton, Hugh Dalton, R. A. Butler, Henry Willink, Robert Hudson, Leathers, Llewellin, Jowitt, Duncan Sandys, Gwilym Lloyd George, Brendan Bracken, Selborne, W. S. Morrison, Ernest Brown, Harry Crookshank, Richard Law, Harold Macmillan, Altrincham, Balfour, Ben Smith, Cherwell, Walter Womersley, Donald Somervell, James Reid, David Maxwell Fyfe, David King Murray, George Hall, James Stuart, William Whiteley, Osbert Peake, William John, Nevil Beechman, Cedric Drewe, Patrick Buchan-Hepburn, Robert Cary, George Tomlinson, Malcolm McCorquodale, George Garro-Jones, Munster, Ellen Wilkinson, Paul Emrys-Evans, Listowel, Devonshire, Bruntisfield, J. P. L. Thomas, Richard Pilkington, Croft, Arthur Henderson, Quintin Hogg, Sherwood, Joseph Westwood, Allan Chapman, John Wilmot, James de Rothschild, Alan Lennox-Boyd, Robert Perkins, Charles Waterhouse, Spencer Summers, James Chuter Ede, Florence Horsbrugh, Tom Williams, Norfolk, Philip Noel-Baker, William Mabane, Charles Peat, George Hicks, Geoffrey*

Lloyd, Tom Smith, Ernest Thurtle, Dingle Foot, Robert Grimston, Wilfred Paling, Sandford, George Mathers, Arthur Young, Fortescue, Alness, Clifden, Normanby, Charles Edwards, Thomas Dugdale, William Boulton, John McEwen, Brabazon, Richard Casey, Duff Cooper, Ronald Cross, Arthur Greenwood, David Grenfell, Hankey, Malcolm MacDonald, Margesson, Portal, Reith, Caldecote, Henry Scrymgeour-Wedderburn, Arthur Salter, Harold Nicholson, Geoffrey Shakespeare, Frederick Montague, Austin Hudson. Added were the following names: *Alanbrook, Cunningham of Hyndhope, Portal of Hungerford, Alexander of Tunis, Edward Bridges, Montgomery of Alamein, Mountbatten, Jan Smuts, William Mackenzie King, Admiral Pound.*

Obverse:
Inscription in oak wreath: SALUTE THE / GREAT COALITION / 1940-1945

Reverse:
Inscription in oak wreath: TO (engraved name) FROM / WINSTON CHURCHILL

Collections:
Marquess of Bath, Chartwell, National Maritime Museum (Admiral of the Fleet Lord Cunningham of Hyndhope's medal)

issue but the amount actually cast was less than fifty; these were without the circular base of the first issue. The rim of the second issue records the particular cast out of the fifty authorized.

Obverse:
Bust of Churchill to left. Legendless. Truncation: KOVACS

Reverse:
Uniface

Collections:
Engstrom

14 Churchill War Coalition Presentation Medal for King George VI, 1946

By WINSTON S. CHURCHILL, United Kingdom

Emitted by Winston S. Churchill, London

Struck by Spink & Son, Ltd., London
A. Æ 112 mm.   1

This medal was prepared at Churchill's instruction for presentation to H.M. King George VI in commemoration of the great wartime coalition cabinet and government which lasted from 1940 to 1945. The medal used the obverse design of the bronze medal presented by Churchill to senior members of the coalition government, but has a unique reverse dedicated to the King. The medal, ordered in December, 1945, was delivered in August, 1946. The former Prime Minister presented the King with the medal in November. It was not until 1951 that Churchill returned as Prime Minister to serve, again, his war-time sovereign. The medal design and inscriptions were of Churchill's own creation.

Obverse:
Inscription in oak wreath. Legend: SALUTE THE / GREAT COALITION / 1940-1945

Reverse:
Inscription in oak wreath. Legend: TO / THE KING / FROM / HIS FAITHFUL / AND DEVOTED SERVANT / WINSTON S. CHURCHILL

Collections:
Royal Collection Windsor Castle, British Museum (electrotype)

15 Churchill Commemorative Plaque, 1949

By FRANK KOVACS, United Kingdom

Emitted by Spink & Son, Ltd., London

Cast by Spink & Son, Ltd., London
A. Æ 133 mm.   50 uniface casts (mounted on circular base)
B. Æ 133 mm.   50 uniface casts (edge numbered)

This fine Churchill portrait of high relief was first produced in 1949 in a limited issue of fifty or less. In 1965, there was a new

16 Churchill Commemorative Medal, 1953

By COSTANTINO AFFER, Italy

Emitted by Costantino Affer, Milan

Cast by the Villani Foundry, Milan
A. Æ 110 mm.   5 uniface casts

This superb and important portrait medal was modelled by the artist in 1953 and was shown at the Exhibition of European Medals, 1930-1955 held at the Royal Society of Arts, London, in June, 1955.

The work has no masters and few peers in Churchillian portraiture in medallic art. Velia Johnson writing in *Italia Numismatica* in June, 1968 commented on this medal:

"The 'Churchill' in the Sheffield Museum is significant in this sense: the powerful and imperious head of the English statesman, logically modelled in the style of the classical Roman coinage, is reminiscent of the era of Vespasian and Titus. But above all there is also visible the naturalistic Donatellian influence—as after the fascinating miracle which is the head of 'Gattamelata' of Padua—imprisoning for all time a brooding soul aware of its dominating strength".

Obverse:
Head of Churchill facing, slightly to left, after the Karsh photographic portrait of 1941. Legend: WINSTON CHURCHILL Truncation: AFFER

Reverse:
Uniface

Collections:
Affer, Engstrom, Sheffield City Museum

17 Churchill Eightieth Birthday Commemorative Medal, 1954

United Kingdom

Emitted by the Conservative Association, London

Struck by The Mint, Birmingham, Ltd., Birmingham

A. Æ 37 mm.   .925   23.5 grms.
B. Æ 37 mm.

Obverse:
Bust of Churchill facing, slightly to left. Legendless

Reverse:
Inscriptional type, two oak branches above, crossed laurel branches below. Legend in center: 1874-1954 / TO / COMMEMORATE / THE 80th BIRTHDAY OF / THE RIGHT HONOURABLE / SIR WINSTON CHURCHILL / K.G., O.M., C.H. / BRITAIN'S WARTIME LEADER / NEVER WAS SO MUCH / OWED BY SO MANY

Collections:
Engstrom

18   Churchill Retirement from the Premiership Commemorative Medal, 1955

United Kingdom

Emitted by the Conservative Association, London

Struck by The Mint, Birmingham, Ltd., Birmingham
A. Æ 37 mm.   .925   23.5 grms.
B. Æ 37 mm.

This medal uses the obverse of the preceding piece. Both medals were distributed by the Conservative Association to commemorate Churchill's eightieth birthday in 1954 and his retirement from the position of Prime Minister the next year.

Obverse:
Bust of Churchill facing, slightly to left. Legendless

Reverse:
Inscriptional type, two oak branches above, crossed laurel branches below legend in center. Legend: BRITAIN'S LEADER IN PEACE & WAR Legend in center: NEVER / WAS SO MUCH / OWED BY SO MANY / THE RIGHT HONOURABLE / SIR WINSTON S. CHURCHILL / K.G., O.M., C.H. / TO MARK HIS RETIREMENT / FROM THE PREMIERSHIP / 5th APRIL 1955

19   Churchill Second World War Leader Commemorative Medal, 1957

By REMO CADEMARTORI and PEDRO CENTENO-VALLENILLA, Venezuela

Emitted by Banco Italo-Venezolano, Caracas and Deutsche Numismatik, Frankfurt-on-Main.

Struck by Acuñaciones C.A., Caracas, and the German State Mint, Karlsruhe
A. N 30 mm.   .900   15 grms.
B. N 21 mm.   .900   6 grms.
C. N 14 mm.   .900   1.5 grms.
D. Æ 30 mm.   .999   13 grms.

Originally issued in 1957, the medal is one of a series of twenty pieces "Jefes en la Segunda Guerra" depicting the Allied and Axis political and military leaders. The medal set has been issued in a number of countries in various weights and finenesses.

Obverse:
Head of Churchill facing, slightly to right. Legend: JEFES EN LA SEGUNDA GUERRA / CHIEFS IN THE SECOND WAR 1939 1945 CHURCHILL Left Field: G. BRT. Right Field: G.B. Truncation: R.B. (sic)

Reverse:
Open-winged condor, talons grasping a sword. Legend: JEFES EN LA SEGUNDA GUERRA / CHIEFS IN THE SECOND WAR BANCO / ITALO-VENEZOLANO / 27 GR. DE ORO PURO · VENEZUELA 1957 · 27 GR. FINE GOLD Left Field: ORO GR. / 30 / LEY 900 / R.C. Right Field: 1939 / 1945 / P.C.-V.

Collections:
Marquess of Bath, Engstrom, Oslo

20   Churchill and the 1940 Club Commemorative Medal, 1959

By FRANK KOVACS, United Kingdom

Emitted by William Maxwell Aitken, Lord Beaverbrook, London

Struck by Spink & Son, Ltd., London
A. N 57 mm.   .375   44
B. Æ gilt 57 mm.   .999   2

This medal was commissioned by Lord Beaverbrook in honor of Churchill and the other members of the "1940 Club" organized by Beaverbrook for all those who had been close to him during his time as Minister of Aircraft Production, a position which he accepted at the urging of his old friend Churchill and in which he served from 1940 to 1941. The "1940 Club" dined together annually at Claridge's and it was one of the few functions that Churchill attended regularly in his last years. The medals were presented to members of the club by Beaverbrook at the 1959 dinner; the portrait commemorated Churchill's eighty-fifth birthday.

Obverse:
Bust of Churchill facing, slightly to left. after the Karsh photographic portrait of 1941. Legend: 1940 CLUB Truncation: FK Exergue: CHURCHILL / MASTER MEMBER / BEAVERBROOK, PRESIDENT

Reverse:
Airplane propeller in center, oak wreath below. Legend: MINISTRY OF AIRCRAFT PRODUCTION. Center Field: "TO WHOM / MUST THE / PRAISE BE GIVEN?" / 23rd MARCH 1941. Below the propeller was engraved the name of the recipient of the medal

Collections:
Marquess of Bath, Engstrom

21 Churchill Second World War Leader Twentieth Anniversary Commemorative Medal, 1959

By RAIMONDO GALDINI, Italy

Emitted by ARGOR S.A., Chiasso, Switzerland, and Euronummus, Milan

Struck by ARGOR S.A., Chiasso

A.	N 32 mm.	.900	18 grms.	} 3000
B.	N 21 mm.	.900	7 grms.	
C.	R 32 mm.	.999	16 grms.	1 (trial strike)

This medal is one of a set of twenty entitled "I Protagonisti" which portray the Allied and Axis leaders of the Second World War, and issued in commemoration of the twentieth anniversary of the war's beginning.

Obverse:
Bust of Churchill to left, Legend: SECONDE GUERRE · SECOND WAR 1939-1945 CHURCHILL Left Field: GRANDE / BRETAGNE Right Field: GREAT / BRITAIN Reeded edge

Reverse:
Mars, sword drawn, standing facing, head to left. Behind are two hemispheric maps of the globe, symbolizing the world conflict wrought by the war. Legend: INT. NUMISMATICS ESTABLISHMENT Exergue: ARGOR 900 / 000

Collections:
Marquess of Bath, Engstrom

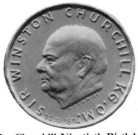

22 Churchill Ninetieth Birthday Commemorative Medal, 1964

By R. SCHMIDT, Austria

Emitted by Gesellschaft für Münzen und Medaillen, Vienna

Struck by the Austrian Mint, Vienna

A.	N 50 mm.	.900	50 grms.	1000
B.	N 32 mm.	.900	17.5 grms.	5000
C.	N 20 mm.	.900	3.5 grms.	6770
D.	R 32 mm.	.999	15 grms.	1 (trial strike)

Obverse:
Head of Churchill to left. Legend: SIR WINSTON CHURCHILL 30.11.1874 Truncation: R. SCHMIDT

Reverse:
Lion to left, guarding Union Jack shield. Arms of the Duke of Marlborough in the left field. Sprig of olive in the exergue. Legend: WE NEVER (sic) SHALL SURRENDER.

Collections:
Marquess of Bath, Engstrom

23 Churchill Ninetieth Birthday Commemorative Medal, 1964

By CHRISTOPHER IRONSIDE, United Kingdom

Emitted by Gesellschaft für Münzen und Medaillen, Vienna

Struck by the Austrian Mint, Vienna

A.	N 50 mm.	.900	50 grms.	1000
B.	N 32 mm.	.900	17.5 grms.	5000
C.	N 20 mm.	.900	3.5 grms.	10,725
D.	R gilt 50 mm.	.999	45 grms.	1000
E.	N 32 mm.	.999	15 grms.	1 (trial strike)

Obverse:
Head of Churchill to left. Legend: · SIR WINSTON CHURCHILL K.G. · O.M. · 30 NOVEMBER 1874 Truncation: IRONSIDE

Reverse:
Rampant lion to left, holding a standard with Union Jack pennant. Legend: · THIS WAS THEIR FINEST HOUR · Exergue: C ·

Collections:
Marquess of Bath, Chartwell, Engstrom

24 Churchill Ninetieth Birthday Commemorative Medal, 196

By WILLEM VIS, Netherlands

Emitted by Koninklijke Begeer N.V., Voorschoten

Struck by Koninklijke Begeer N.V., Voorschoten

A.	N 50 mm.	.900	90 grms.	250*
B.	N 38 mm.	.900	50 grms.	2000*
C.	N 30 mm.	.900	15 grms.	
D.	N 25 mm.	.900	8 grms.	
E.	N 22 mm.	.900	7 grms.	
F.	N 18 mm.	.900	4 grms.	
G.	R 50 mm.	.925		
H.	R 38 mm.	.925		
I.	R 30 mm.	.925		
J.	R 25 mm.	.925		
K.	R 22 mm.	.925		
L.	R 18 mm.	.925		
M.	Æ 50 mm.			

* (numbered)

Obverse:
Head of Churchill to right, Legend: WINSTON LEONARD SPENCE CHURCHILL 90th BIRTHDAY 30-11-1964. Truncation: WV (f monogram)

Reverse:
Globe, flying dove with olive sprig. Legend: FORWARD UNFLINCH- / ING, UNSWER- / VING, INDOM- / ITABLE, TILL / WHO- / LE TASK / IS DONE / AND THE WHO- / LE WORLD IS / SA AND / CLEAN. Left Field: WINSTON CHURCHILL / WORLD BROADCAST / MAY 1945

Collections:
A.N.S., Marquess of Bath, Engstrom

Churchill Ninetieth Birthday Commemorative Medal, 1964

REMO CADEMARTORI, Venezuela

Emitted by Deutsche Numismatik, Frankfurt-on-Main

Struck by the German State Mint, Karlsruhe

N	30 mm.	.986	17.5 grms.	50*
R	30 mm.	.999	13 grms.	1000*

(numbered)

Issued to commemorate Churchill's ninetieth birthday, this medal combines the obverse of the 1957 "Jefes en la Segunda Guerre" Churchill medal with a special reverse; the issue was limited. For some later strikings the reverse die was changed to a MCMLXV date to make the medal a memorial piece following Churchill's death.

Obverse:
Head of Churchill facing, slightly to right. Legend: JEFES EN LA SEGUNDA GUERRA / CHIEFS IN THE SECOND WAR 1939 1945 CHURCHILL Left Field: G. BRT. Right Field: G.B. Truncation: B. (sic)

Reverse:
Inscriptional type in laurel wreath, date in small rectangular tablet. Legend: CUSUS / UT MEMORIA / VIVAT MCMLXIV (Struck as a Lasting Memorial, 1964) Exergue: SILBER 1000 FEIN CA 13 G.

Collections:
N.S., Marquess of Bath, Engstrom

Churchill Memorial Medal, 1965

ANDREW ANDRECHUK, Canada.

Emitted by Wellings Manufacturing Company, Ltd., Toronto, Ontario

Struck by the Wellings Manufacturing Company, Ltd., Toronto, Ontario

N	52 mm.	.999	182.5 grms.	10*
R	52 mm.	.999	155.5 grms.	1000*
Æ	52 mm.			10,000

(numbered)

The medal designs were suggested by Mr. and Mrs. Fred A. Rhode, the portrait was modelled by Andrew Andrechuk, and the dies engraved by Ben Ireland. The medal was the first Churchill memorial medal to appear, being issued on January , 1965, three days after Sir Winston's death.

Obverse:
Bust of Churchill facing, slightly to left, after the Karsh photographic portrait of 1941. Legend: SIR WINSTON CHURCHILL Truncation: BI AA (monogram)

Reverse:
Crossed British and Canadian flags, at half-mast, forming a

"V for Victory" sign, and Churchill's own words for the legend. Legend in center: IN WAR: RESOLUTION / IN VICTORY: MAGNANIMITY / IN DEFEAT: DEFIANCE / IN PEACE: GOODWILL / SIR WINSTON CHURCHILL / NOVEMBER 30, 1874 / JANUARY 24, 1965

Collections:
Marquess of Bath, Engstrom

27   Churchill Memorial Medal, 1965

By S. G. M. ADAMS, United Kingdom

Emitted by M. & E. Adams, Jewellery Manufacturers, Leeds

Struck by M. & E. Adams, Jewellery Manufacturers, Leeds

A.	N	25 mm.	.999	15 grms.	300
B.	R	25 mm.	.999	8.5 grms.	300
C.	Æ	25 mm.			25
D.	Brass	25 mm.			25
E.	Alum.	25 mm.			25

This piece was the first British memorial medal to appear following Churchill's death. It was struck one week after Churchill's death. The artist hand-engraved the dies directly without using a reducing machine.

Obverse:
Bust of Churchill in "siren suit" to left. Legendless. Truncation: S.G. (for Samuel George—the artist's first names)

Reverse:
Inscriptional type. Legend: SIR / WINSTON / CHURCHILL / 1874-1965   Exergue: M.A. (monogram, for Meyers Adams—continuation of the artist's name from the obverse truncation)

Collections:
Marquess of Bath, Engstrom

N.B.—The artist muled his obverse die of the above medal with several other dies of medals he had previously produced, thus creating a very large number of varieties for this medal, and for his subsequent Churchill medals which were also muled with these and other dies. The varieties are listed as sub-types of the major portrait die for all the Adams' Churchill medals.

27-I

Obverse:
Bust of Churchill in "siren suit" to left. Legendless. Truncation: S.G.

Reverse:
Bust of R.A.F. pilot to left. Legend: BATTLE OF BRITAIN 25th ANNIVERSARY (Obverse from a 1965 medal, the reverse of which is below)

A.	R	25 mm.	.999	8.5 grms.	6
B.	Copper	25 mm.			6

27-II

Obverse:
Bust of Churchill in "siren suit" to left. Legendless. Truncation: S.G.

Reverse:
Flying facing eagle, wings spread. Below, a V-shaped flight of nine Spitfire fighters. Legend: 1940-1965

A. Æ 25 mm.   .999   8.5 grms.   6
B. Copper 25 mm.   6

27-V

Obverse:
Bust of Churchill in "siren suit" to left. Legendless. Truncation S.G.

Reverse:
Triskelion shield. Legend: 1765-1965 ISLE OF MAN

A. Æ 25 mm.   .999   8.5 grms.   6
B. Copper 25 mm.   6

27-III

Obverse:
Bust of Churchill in "siren suit" to left. Legendless. Truncation: S.G.

Reverse:
Westminster Abbey. Legend: WESTMINSTER ABBEY 900 YEARS CONSECRATED 28 DEC. 1065

A. Æ 25 mm.   .999   8.5 grms.   4
B. Copper 25 mm.   4

27-VI

Obverse:
Bust of Churchill in "siren suit" to left. Legendless. Truncatio S.G.

Reverse:
Bust of King Edward VIII to left. Legend: EDWARD · VIII KING · & · EMPEROR

A. Æ 25 mm.   .999   8.5 grms.   6
B. Nickel 25 mm.   6
C. Brass 25 mm.   6
D. Copper 25 mm.   6

Collections:
Marquess of Bath

27-IV

Obverse:
Bust of Churchill in "siren suit" to left. Legendless. Truncation: S.G.

Reverse:
Crowned cypher. Legend: BICENTENARY OF THE REVESTMENT ACT · 1765. (Obverse from a 1965 medal, the reverse of which is below)

A. Æ 25 mm.   .999   8.5 grms.   6
B. Copper 25 mm.   6

27-VII

Obverse:
Bust of Churchill in "siren suit" to left. Legendless. Truncatio S.G.

Reverse:
Bust of President John F. Kennedy to left. Legend: JOHN KENNEDY 1917-1963

A. Æ 25 mm.   .999   8.5 grms.   4
B. Copper 25 mm.   4

Collections:
Marquess of Bath

27-VIII

Obverse:
Bust of Churchill in "siren suit" to left. Legendless. Truncation: S.G.

Reverse:
Bust of Dr. Albert Schweitzer to left. Legend: 1875-DR. ALBERT SCHWEITZER-1965

A.	Æ 25 mm.	.999	8.5 grms.	6
B.	Copper 25 mm.			6

Collections:
Marquess of Bath

27-IX

Obverse:
Bust of Churchill in "siren suit" to left. Legendless. Truncation: S.G.

Reverse:
Uniface. Engraved Legend: SIR / WINSTON / CHURCHILL / 30 · 11 · 1874

A.	Æ 25 mm.	.999	8.5 grms.	4
B.	Copper 25 mm.			4

Collections:
Marquess of Bath

29 Churchill Memorial Medal, 1965

By COSTANTINO AFFER, Italy

Emitted by Euronummus, Milan

Struck by Euronummus, Milan

A.	N 40 mm.	.900	30 grms.	500
B.	N 30 mm.	.900	15 grms.	500
C.	N 25 mm.	.900	7.5 grms.	1150
D.	N 21 mm.	.900	4 grms.	1200
E.	Æ gilt 40 mm.		19 grms.	(trial strikes)

Obverse:
Bust of Churchill facing, slightly to left, after the Karsh photographic portrait of 1941. Legend SIR WINSTON CHURCHILL — 1874 · 1965 — Truncation: AFFER Pellet ring, reeded edge.

Reverse:
Churchill's right hand in victory sign; behind, a lion passant and four allied flags: American, Russian, French and British. Pellet ring. Exergue: .900 VICTORY (on E Right Field: PROVA)

Collections:
Marquess of Bath, Engstrom

28 Churchill Memorial Medal, 1965

By S. G. M. ADAMS, United Kingdom

Emitted by M. & E. Adams, Jewellery Manufacturers, Leeds

Struck by M. & E. Adams, Jewellery Manufacturers, Leeds

A.	N 20 mm.	.999	10 grms.	30
B.	N 20 mm.	.750	7 grms.	20
C.	N 20 mm.	.375	4 grms.	20
D.	Æ 20 mm.	.999	3 grms.	50
E.	Æ 20 mm.			3
F.	Brass 20 mm.			3
G.	Copper 20 mm.			3
H.	Alum. 20 mm.			25

This medal was the second British memorial piece to appear following Churchill's death. It followed the previous medal by the same artist by one week, and was struck two weeks after Churchill's death.

Obverse:
Bust of Churchill in "siren suit" to left. Legendless.

Reverse:
Inscriptional type, laurel wreath below, Legend in Center: SIR / WINSTON / CHURCHILL / 1874-1965 Exergue: M.A. (Meyers Adams)

Collections:
Marquess of Bath, Engstrom

30 Churchill Memorial Medal, 1965

By FRANK KOVACS, United Kingdom

Emitted by Spink & Son, Ltd., London

Struck by Spink & Son, Ltd., London

A.	N 56 mm.	.916	135 grms.	500*
B.	N 39 mm.	.916	47 grms.	1000*
C.	Æ 56 mm.	.925	81 grms.	
D.	Æ 39 mm.	.925	28 grms.	

* (numbered)

This fine original medal was issued in a special set of the first hundred of A and B.

Obverse:
Bust of Churchill facing, slightly to left, after the Karsh photographic portrait of 1941. In the background is a shelf, with books to the left and paint brushes to the right, to symbolize Churchill's distinction as an author and artist. Exergue: WINSTON CHURCHILL / 1874-1965 Truncation: KOVACS

Reverse:
Defiant soldier with raised fist guarding England's shores, a tempestuous channel around, flight of enemy airplanes above. (Adapted from the famous cartoon by Sir David Low published in the *Evening Standard* in 1940 following the evacuation from Dunkirk and the beginning of the Battle of Britain). Exergue: "VERY WELL, ALONE" Truncation: LOW, DES. SPINK, FEC.

Collections:
A.N.S., Marquess of Bath, Engstrom

31 Churchill Memorial Medal, 1965

By RALPH J. MENCONI, United States

Emitted by Presidential Art Medals Inc., Englewood, Ohio

Struck by Medallic Art Company, New York City
A. Æ 63 mm.   .999   163 grms.   2500*
B. Æ 70 mm.
*(numbered)

Obverse:
Bust of Churchill facing, after the Karsh photographic portrait
of 1941. Legend: SIR WINSTON CHURCHILL Left Field: 1874 /
1965 Truncation: RALPH J. MENCONI / ©1965 PAM

Reverse:
Seal of the royal arms of the United Kingdom, right foreground.
Smaller seal of the United States in left foreground. Behind,
the Houses of Parliament, clouds above. The legendless reverse
symbolizes three of Churchill's greatest areas of achievement:
Parliament, where he served a life-time as a "child of the
House of Commons", the five sovereigns of the United Kingdom
and the British Commonwealth whom he served, the United
States which knew him as the son of an American mother, an
ever-faithful ally and friend, and finally, by a special act of
Congress in 1963, as an honorary citizen.

Collections:
A.N.S., Ashmolean, Marquess of Bath, British Museum,
Engstrom, Smithsonian Institution

32 Churchill Memorial Medal, 1965

By HARALD SALOMON, Denmark

Emitted by Harald Salomon, Copenhagen

Cast by Nic. Outzon Schmidt, Copenhagen
A. Æ 95 mm.   3 casts

This excellent portrait piece by the Royal Danish Mint Medalist
was modelled soon after Churchill's death as an expression of
admiration. The artist commented: "I was inspired to make the
medal after the death of Sir Winston Churchill as a commemoration of his work to free humanity from the scourge of Nazism
and his life's work for peace on earth". The medal was shown at
the F.I.D.E.M. exhibition in Paris in 1967.

Obverse:
Bust of Churchill in "siren suit" facing, slightly to right.
Legend: WINSTON CHURCHILL Left Field: HS (monogram)

Reverse:
Churchill's right hand in "V for Victory" sign. Legend: (star)
30 · 11 · 1874 (cross) 24 · 1 · 1965

Collections:
Marquess of Bath, Engstrom, Salomon

33 Churchill Memorial Medal, 1965

By COSTANTINO AFFER, Italy

Emitted by the Metalimport Group, London, and Euronummus,
Milan

Struck by Johnson, Matthey & Co., Ltd., London, and Euro-
nummus, Milan
A. N 40 mm.   .916   30 grms.   500*
B. N 30 mm.   .916   15 grms.   500*
C. N 25 mm.   .916   7.5 grms.   500*
D. N 21 mm.   .916   4 grms.   500*
E. N 40 mm.   .750   30 grms.   2500*
F. N 30 mm.   .750   15 grms.   3000*
G. N 25 mm.   .750   7.5 grms.   3500*
H. N 21 mm.   .750   4 grms.   4000*
I. Æ 40 mm.   .960   34 grms.   1000*
* (numbered)

Medals A to D were issued as sets only. The first one thousand
of E to H were issued as sets. The medal is based on the same
design as entry 28. In fact, medals A to D were struck in Milan
with the beaded border dies, while E to I are from the dies with
Morse code border, struck in London.

Obverse:
Bust of Churchill facing, slightly to left, after the Karsh photographic portrait of 1941. Legend: SIR WINSTON CHURCHILL —
1874 · 1965 — Truncation: AFFER. The border ring consists of
the Morse code victory signal " . . . —" used on the B.B.C.
during the war and taken from the first notes of Beethoven's
Fifth Symphony.

Reverse:
Churchill's right hand in victory sign; behind, a lion passant
and four allied flags: American, Russian, French and British.
Victory Morse code signal border ring. Exergue: VICTORY

Collections:
Marquess of Bath, Engstrom

34 Churchill Memorial Medal, 1965

By COSTANTINO AFFER, Italy

Emitted by SIROM, Milan

Struck by SIROM, Milan
A. N 50 mm.   .900   70 grms.   1000*
B. N 40 mm.   .900   30 grms.
C. N 34 mm.   .900   20 grms.
D. N 27 mm.   .900   10 grms.
E. N 20 mm.   .900   5 grms.
F. Æ gilt 40 mm.   16.5 grms.   (trial strikes)
* (numbered)

Obverse:
Quarter-length figure of Churchill facing, with right hand raised in victory sign, head slightly to left and after the Karsh photographic portrait of 1941. Legend: WINSTON CHURCHILL 1874-1965 (On medal F, Left Field: PROVA)

Reverse:
Face of clock representing "Big Ben"; the hands nearing twelve. Superimposed on the face are the Houses of Parliament and "Big Ben". The clock-face symbolizes "the finest hour" in British history. Left Field: JUNE Right Field: 1940 Exergue: THE FINEST / HOUR

Collections:
Engstrom

Reverse:
Britannia seated to right, with trident and supporting two over-lapping shields; a Union Jack appearing on one, the other shows an American shield with a diagonal scroll inscribed "LIBERTY" with only the last five letters visible. Legend: FRIEND AND HONORARY CITIZEN OF THE UNITED STATES Right Field: CA (monogram) Exergue: IN / MEMORIAM Beaded border

Collections:
A.N.S., Ashmolean, Marquess of Bath, British Museum, Engstrom

35 Churchill Memorial Medal, 1965

By A. LOEWENTAL, United Kingdom

Emitted by B. A. Seaby, Ltd., London

Struck by John Pinches (Medallists) Ltd., London

A.	N	50 mm.	.916	109 grms.	500
B.	N	50 mm.	.375	81 grms.	200
C.	Æ	50 mm.	.958	77.5 grms.	736
D.	Æ	50 mm			1421

This piece is a re-issue of the 1945 Loewental medal in reduced size and with the addition of the death date (12). The dies were presented to the British Museum.

Obverse:
Bust of Churchill to left. Legend: CHURCHILL, Left Field: 1945 (Victory sign incuse, date superimposed), Truncation: A. LOEWENTAL / LINCOLN / OB. 24. JAN. 1965.

Reverse:
Hand, rising from cloud, holding victory torch. Legend: · UNFLINCHING · INDOMITABLE · HIS · SPIRIT · SAVED · BRITAIN · AND · SO · THE · WORLD · Left and Right Fields: WE · WILL FIGHT · ON / LAND ON · SEA / AND · IN THE · AIR / UNTIL VICTORY IS WON. Exergue: AL (incuse monogram)

Collections:
Marquess of Bath, British Museum, Engstrom, Smithsonian Institution

36 Churchill Memorial Medal, 1965

By C. M. CASTO, United States

Emitted by Commemorative Arts, Mineral Springs, West Virginia

Struck by Wendell's, Minneapolis, Minnesota

A.	Æ	40 mm.	.925	30 grms.	200*
B.	Goldine	40 mm.			1000
C.	Æ	40 mm.			1000

* (numbered)

The piece was the third medal in the "Current Events Series" of the issuer. The medal honors Churchill as a friend and Honorary Citizen of the U.S.A.

Obverse:
Bust of Churchill facing, slightly left, after the Karsh eightieth birthday photographic portrait, 1954. Legend: SIR WINSTON SPENCER CHVRCHILL 1874-1965 Beaded border.

37 Churchill Memorial Medal, 1965

By WIESLAW ANTONI PATER and EDGAR JOHN KOHLER, United Kingdom

Emitted by Toye, Kenning & Spencer Ltd., London

Struck by W. J. Dingley Ltd., Birmingham

A.	N	57 mm.	.916	109.5 grms.	500*
B.	N	38 mm.	.916	38 grms.	1000*
C.	Æ gilt	57 mm.	.925	65 grms.	1000
D.	Æ gilt	38 mm.	.925	24 grms.	1000
E.	Æ	57 mm.	.925	65 grms.	2500
F.	Æ	38 mm.	.925	24 grms.	1500
G.	Æ	57 mm.			6000
H.	Æ	38 mm.			5000

* (numbered)

Two hundred sets of A and B were issued.

Obverse:
Bust of Churchill, slightly to left, after an eightieth birthday photographic portrait, 1954. No legend. Truncation: E.K.

Reverse:
Churchill family arms shield with the Garter. Legend: THE Rt HON. SIR WINSTON SPENCER-CHURCHILL. K.G, O.M. C.H. 1874 1965

Collections:
Marquess of Bath, Engstrom

38 Churchill Memorial Medal, 1965

By WIESLAW ANTONI PATER and EDGAR JOHN KOHLER, United Kingdom

Emitted by John Taylor (Silversmiths) Ltd., London

Struck by W. J. Dingley Ltd., Birmingham

A.	N	57 mm.	.916	109.5 grms.	500*
B.	N	38 mm.	.916	38 grms.	500*
C.	Æ gilt	57 mm.	.925	65 grms.	1000
D.	Æ gilt	38 mm.	.925	24 grms.	1000
E.	Æ	57 mm.	.925	65 grms.	1000
F.	Æ	38 mm.	.925	24 grms.	1000

G. Æ 57 mm. 5000
H. Æ 38 mm. 5000

The issuing firm is an associated company of Toye, Kenning & Spencer Ltd. and it used the same obverse as the parent company's medal for this piece but with a distinct reverse. W. A. Pater designed the medal, and the modelling was by E. J. Kohler. Sets of all metals in each size were issued.

Obverse:
Bust of Churchill facing, slightly to left, after an eightieth birthday photographic portrait, 1954. No legend. Truncation: E.K.

Reverse:
Inscription, laurel wreath below. Legend in Center: THE RT. HON. / SIR / WINSTON / SPENCER-CHURCHILL, / K.G., O.M., C.H. / 1874-1965

Collections:
A.N.S., Marquess of Bath, Engstrom

39 Churchill Memorial Medal, 1965
By LESLIE E. PINCHES, United Kingdom
Emitted by John Pinches (Medallists) Ltd., London
Struck by John Pinches (Medallists) Ltd., London

A. Platinum 51 mm. .999 140 grms. 50*
B. Platinum 38 mm. .999 60 grms. 50*
C. N 51 mm. .916 105 grms. 500*
D. N 38 mm. .916 44 grms. 1000*
E. N 51 mm. .375 81 grms. 500
F. N 38 mm. .375 35 grms. 1000
G. R 51 mm. .958 68 grms.
H. R 38 mm. .958 34 grms.
I. Æ 51 mm.
J. Æ 38 mm. * (numbered)

The first twenty-five numbered medals of A and B were issued as sets.

Obverse:
Bust of Churchill facing, slightly to left, after the Karsh photographic portrait of 1941. Legend: WINSTON CHURCHILL Left Field: 1874 Right Field: 1965 Truncation: L.E. PINCHES (incuse)

Reverse:
Churchill family arms; a shield quartering the arms of Churchill with those of Spencer. The dexter crest is of Churchill, and the sinister crest is of Spencer. The motto on the scroll is FIEL PERO DESDICHADO (Faithful Though Unfortunate). The Garter appears around the shield.

Collections:
Marquess of Bath, Engstrom

40 Churchill Crown Commemorative Medal, 1965
By BRUNO CAVALLO, Canada
Emitted by the Canadian Centennial Numismatic Park, Sudbury, Ontario
Struck by Wellings Manufacturing Company Ltd., Toronto, Ontario

A. R 41 mm. .999 47 grms. 225*
B. Nickel-R 41 mm. 47 grms.
C. Æ 41 mm.
* (numbered)

Obverse:
Quarter-length figure of Churchill facing with left hand raised in victory sign, head slightly to left after the Karsh photographic portrait of 1941. Legend: SIR WINSTON CHURCHILL (star) 1874 (cross) 1965 Truncation: BC

Reverse:
Churchill family arms, depiction of the Churchill Crown memorial. Legend: CANADIAN CENTENNIAL NUMISMATIC PARK Right and Left Fields: CHURCHILL / 5 SHILLINGS / COIN / MEMORIAL / 1965 Exergue: B · I (Ben Irwin, die engraver) SUDBURY * CANADA / WELLINGS

Collections:
A.N.S., Marquess of Bath, Engstrom

41 Churchill Memorial Medal, 1965
By S. G. M. ADAMS, United Kingdom
Emitted by M. & E. Adams, Jewellery Manufacturers, Leeds
Struck by M. & E. Adams, Jewellery Manufacturers, Leeds

A. N 32 mm. .999 23 grms. 3
B. R 32 mm. .999 17 grms. 12
C. Æ 32 mm. 6
D. Alum. 32 mm. 12

Another medal in the series by the artist, this piece was produced in trial strikes until the dies broke. The artist worked without use of a plaster cast or reducing machine as with his other works.

Obverse:
Bust of Churchill in military uniform to left. Legend: WINSTON S. CHURCHILL

Reverse:
Lion in defiant attitude to left upon a rocky ground. Legend: GREAT BRITAIN

Collections:
Marquess of Bath, Engstrom.

N.B.—The artist muled this obverse die with several other dies from other medals creating many varieties with the same portrait obverse die.

41-I

Obverse:
Bust of Churchill in military uniform to left. Legend: WINSTON
S. CHURCHILL

Reverse:
Passant heraldic lion to left.
A. Æ 32 mm. .999 17 grms. 2
B. Copper 32 mm. 2

Collections:
Marquess of Bath

41-II

Obverse:
Bust of Churchill in military uniform to left. Legend: WINSTON
S. CHURCHILL

Reverse:
Britannia seated to left. Legend: BRITANNIA
A. Æ 32 mm. .999 17 grms. 2
B. Copper 32 mm. 2

Collections:
Marquess of Bath

41-III

Obverse:
Bust of Churchill in military uniform to left. Legend: WINSTON
S. CHURCHILL

Reverse:
Bust of Joseph Stalin to left. Legend: J. V. STALIN
A. Æ 32 mm. .999 17 grms. 4
B. Copper 32 mm. 2

Collections:
Marquess of Bath, Engstrom

41-IV

Obverse:
Bust of Churchill in military uniform to left. Legend: WINSTON
S. CHURCHILL

Reverse:
Kirkstall Abbey in Yorkshire. Legend: KIRKSTALL ABBEY
A. Æ 32 mm. .999 17 grms. 4
B. Copper 32 mm. 2

Collections:
Marquess of Bath

41-V

Obverse:
Bust of Churchill in military uniform to left. Legend: WINSTON
S. CHURCHILL

Reverse:
Design after the last farthing coin with wren and legend. Legend:
1956 FARTHING
A. Æ 32 mm. .999 17 grms. 4
B. Copper 2

Collections:
Marquess of Bath

41-VI

Obverse:
Bust of Churchill in military uniform to left. Legend: WINSTON
S. CHURCHILL

Reverse:
Bust of King Edward VIII to left. Legend: EDWARD · VIII ·
KING · & · EMPEROR (Obverse of the following medal).
A. Æ 32 mm. .999 17 grms. 4
B. Copper 32 mm. 2

Collections:
Marquess of Bath

41-VII

Obverse:
Bust of Churchill in military uniform to left. Legend: WINSTON
S. CHURCHILL

Reverse:
Mounted St. George to left, slaying dragon. Legend on scroll:
1936 (Reverse from the above medal).

| A. | Æ 32 mm. | .999 | 17 grms. | 4 |
| B. | Copper 32 mm. | | | 2 |

Collections:
Marquess of Bath

41-VIII

Obverse:
Bust of Churchill in military uniform to left. Legend: WINSTON S. CHURCHILL

Reverse:
Uniface. Engraved Legend: STATESMAN / AND / AUTHOR / 1874-1965

| A. | Æ 32 mm. | .999 | 17 grms. | 2 |

Collections:
Marquess of Bath

41-IX

Obverse:
Bust of Churchill in military uniform to left. Legend: WINSTON S. CHURCHILL

Reverse:
Bust of H.R.H. the Duke of Windsor, three-quarters left. Legend: H.R.H. THE DUKE OF WINDSOR

| A. | Æ 32 mm. | .999 | 17 grms. | 1 |

42   Churchill Memorial Medal, 1965

By EMMANUEL HAHN and ELIZABETH WYNWOOD, Canada

Emitted by the Canada Medal & Token Company, Aurora, Ontario

Struck by Canadian Artistic Dies, Inc., Sherbrooke, Quebec

A.	Æ gilt 38 mm.	.999	47 grms.	31
B.	Æ 38 mm.	.999	47 grms.	100
C.	Goldine 38 mm.			500
D.	Æ 38 mm.			1550

The designs for the medal were suggested by Roderick V. Smith of the Canada Medal & Token Company. Elizabeth Wynwood Hahn followed the plaster portrait-plaque done by her husband Emmanuel Hahn at the Quebec Conference in 1943. The dies were engraved by Orazio N. Lombardo of Canadian Artistic Dies after Elizabeth Wynwood's models. There are two varieties of the reverse easily distinguishable by the different exergues: C.A.D. or C. ART DIES and by a longer sword on the latter reverse.

Obverse:
Bust of Churchill to right by Elizabeth Wynwood after the Churchill portrait-plaque by Emmanuel Hahn, 1943. Exergue: WINSTON LEONARD SPENCER / CHURCHILL / K.G. P.C. O.M. C.H. Truncation: E.H.

Reverse:
Quill pen and inkstand at right angles to a sword. Legend in Center: ONE WHO BECAME A GOLDEN GLORIOUS / LEGEND IN HIS OWN / LIFETIME / (after the eulogy by the Archbishop of Canterbury at Churchill's funeral, January 30, 1965) (star) 1874 / (cross) 1965 / THE VOICE OF FREEDOM   Truncation: E.W.W. Exergue: C.A.D. or C. ART DIES

Collections:
A.N.S., Ashmolean, Marquess of Bath, British Museum, Engstrom

43   Churchill Memorial Medal, 1965

By HANS DILLER, Germany

Emitted by Münzen und Medaillen Motek Horowicz & Co., Vienna

Struck by the Austrian Mint, Vienna, and the German State Mint, Munich.

A.	N 60 mm.	.900	175 grms.	200
B.	N 60 mm.	.900	140 grms.	300
C.	N 50 mm.	.900	105 grms.	500
D.	N 50 mm.	.900	70 grms.	1500
E.	N 40 mm.	.900	35 grms.	1000
F.	N 32 mm.	.900	17.5 grms.	
G.	N 26 mm.	.900	10.5 grms.	
H.	N 20 mm.	.900	3.5 grms.	
I.	Æ 40 mm.	.999	25 grms.	

Of this powerful portrait medal, A to I were struck at the Munich mint, and in addition E to H were also struck at the Vienna mint.

Obverse:
Head of Churchill to left. Wreath of crossed laurel branches below. Legend: WINSTON CHURCHILL Truncation: HD (monogram)

Reverse:
Inscriptional type within wreath of laurel branches, between two oak leaf clusters. Legend: IN / MEMORIAM / 1874-1965 / (cross)

Collections:
Marquess of Bath, Engstrom

44   Churchill Memorial Plaque, 1965

By BRUNO GALOPPI, Italy

Emitted by Bruno Galoppi, Arezzo

Cast by Bruno Galoppi, Arezzo

| A. | Æ 140 mm. | 4 uniface casts |

This excellent modern portrait-plaque was prepared for exhibition at the Triennale d'Arte di Udine, 1966, at the Italian Mint,

Rome, and later, at the French Mint, Paris. It is a remarkably original treatment of the subject.

Obverse:
Head of Churchill facing, in oval incuse. The face is divided in half by a vertical line separating two contrasting sculpturing techniques employed on the two parts. The left half is a life study in smooth lines; the right half is an impressionistic rough-sculptured study. The two styles are mirrored in the contrast between the raised and incuse letters of the legend which reads vertically. Legend: CHURCHILL (alternating raised and incuse letters) Truncation: B. GALOPPI (incuse)

Reverse:
Uniface

Collections:
Marquess of Bath, Engstrom, Galoppi

45   Churchill Memorial Medal, 1965

By FRANK KOVACS, United Kingdom

Emitted by Gregory & Co. (Jewellers) Ltd., London

Struck by Gregory & Co. (Jewellers) Ltd., London

A.	Platinum 57 mm	.999	172 grms.	15*
B.	Platinum 39 mm	.999	56 grms.	15*
C.	N 57 mm.	.916	137 grms.	500*
D.	N 39 mm.	.916	47 grms.	1000*
E.	N 23 mm.	.916	7.5 grms.	20000*
F.	Æ 57 mm.	.925		5000*
G.	Æ 39 mm.	.925		5000*

* (numbered)

The first two hundred of C and D were issued as sets. Two hundred sets of D and E were also issued, as well as sets of two thousand medals of F and G.

Obverse:
Bust of Churchill facing, slightly to left, after an eightieth birthday photographic portrait, 1954. Legend: · WINSTON SPENCER CHURCHILL · · 1874-1965 · Truncation: KOVACS (incuse)

Reverse:
Churchill's right hand in victory sign. Legendless.

Collections:
Marquess of Bath, Engstrom

46   Churchill and the Battle of Britain 25th Anniversary Commemorative Medal, 1965

By ANTHONY M. FOLEY and KENNETH C. HUNT, United Kingdom

Emitted by The Westminster Mint & Die Co., London

Struck by The Westminster Mint & Die Co., London

A.	N 38 mm.	.916	62 grms.	1000

B.	Æ 38 mm.	.999		5000
C.	Æ 38 mm.			1200

An interesting feature of this medal is the fact that the dies were hand engraved without the use of models or a reducing machine, following the classic technique which has all but disappeared today. Presentation medals were accepted by H.M. Queen Elizabeth II and Lady Churchill.

Obverse:
Bust of Churchill facing, slightly to left, after the Karsh photographic portrait of 1941. Legend: WINSTON LEONARD SPENCER-CHURCHILL Truncation: K. C. HUNT Rim: A. M. FOLEY

Reverse:
Royal Air Force ace pilot A. G. Malan running to his Mark 1A Spitfire airplane, attended by a ground crew. Legend: NOT SO EASILY SHALL THE LIGHTS OF FREEDOM DIE — 1940 — Left Field: K C H Right Field: A. M. FOLEY

Collections:
A.N.S., Marquess of Bath, Chartwell, Engstrom

47   Churchill Memorial Medal, 1965

By PAUL VINCZE, United Kingdom

Emitted by the National Commemorative Society, Philadelphia, Pa.

Struck by the Franklin Mint, Yeadon, Pa.

A.	Platinum 39 mm.	.999		3*
B.	Æ 39 mm.	.925	26 grms.	5249*

* (numbered)

The platinum medal numbered one was presented to Lady Churchill, the second was retained by the society, and the third was presented to the Smithsonian Institution in Washington. The piece is the eleventh medal of the society's issues, and was only distributed to members. The dies have been destroyed.

Obverse:
Bust of Churchill facing, slightly to left, after the Karsh photographic portrait of 1941. Legend: . SIR WINSTON CHURCHILL . 1874-1965 Right Field: P. VINCZE

Reverse:
Two mourning female figures, heads bowed, the left figure holding a United States shield, the right figure holding a British shield. The figures drape a garland above an inscribed tablet. Legend: THE MAN OF THE CENTURY Legend in center: IN WAR / RESOLUTION / IN DEFEAT / DEFIANCE / IN VICTORY / MAGNANIMITY / IN PEACE / GOODWILL Right Field: P. VINCZE Exergue: HONORARY CITIZEN OF / THE UNITED STATES / OF AMERICA / NCS 1965 / FM (monogram)

Collections:
A.N.S., Marquess of Bath, British Museum, Chartwell, Engstrom, Smithsonian Institution

48   Churchill Memorial Medal, 1965

By ORAZIO N. LOMBARDO, Canada

Emitted by Elizron Enterprises, Tillsonburg, Ontario

Struck by Canadian Artistic Dies, Inc., Sherbrooke, Quebec

A.	N	20 mm.	.999		25
B.	N	20 mm.	.585		30
C.	Æ	20 mm.	.999	4.5 grms.	1000
D.	Æ gilt 20 mm.			4.5 grms.	500
E.	Æ	20 mm.			50000

The medal is the second in the "World Personalities Series" of the emitting firm. The designs were suggested by Ralph A. Srigley of Elizron Enterprises, and executed by Orazio N. Lombardo. The reverse legend is a quotation from Churchill's speech to the House on May 13, 1940, upon becoming Prime Minister.

Obverse:
Bust of Churchill in military uniform facing, slightly to left, after a photograph taken in Germany during his inspection tour of March, 1945. Legend: SIR WINSTON CHURCHILL   Left Field: (star) 1874   Right Field: 1965 (cross)

Reverse:
Broad horizontal band intersected by a lighted victory torch, with a central legend. Legend: WITHOUT VICTORY / THERE IS NO / SURVIVAL   Left Field: (rayed star). Exergue: C. ART DIES

Collections:
A.N.S., Ashmolean, Marquess of Bath, British Museum, Engstrom

50   Churchill and the Dunkirk Evacuation 25th Anniversary Commemorative Medal, 1965

By GEOFFREY COLLEY, United Kingdom

Emitted by Slade, Hampton & Son, Ltd., London

Struck by Johnson, Matthey & Co., Ltd., London

A.	Platinum 65 mm.	.999	153 grms.	6*
B.	Platinum 32 mm.	.999	31 grms.	6*
C.	N	65 mm.	.916	105 grms.	1000*
D.	N	32 mm.	.916	17.5 grms.	1500*
E.	Æ	65 mm.	.925	(trial strikes)	
F.	Æ	32 mm.	.925	(trial strikes)	
G.	Æ gilt 65 mm.			(trial strikes)	

* (numbered)

Six sets of A and B were issued. The first five hundred of C and D were issued as correspondingly-numbered sets. The portrait and reverse are nicely rendered by the artist.

Obverse:
Quarter-length figure of Churchill, slightly left, wearing "siren suit". Legend: WE SHALL NEVER SURRENDER   Truncation: G. COLLEY (incuse)

Reverse:
Dunkirk evacuation scene of soldiers on the beach, ships and shell explosions in the background, small bluff in the foreground. Legend: DUNKIRK · 1940   Right Field: G. COLLEY (incuse)

Collections:
A.N.S., Marquess of Bath, Engstrom

49   Churchill Memorial Medal, 1965

By JOSEF HOTTER, United States

Emitted by Federal Brand Enterprises Inc., Cleveland, Ohio

Struck by Federal Brand Enterprises Inc., Cleveland, Ohio

A.	Æ	27 mm.	.900	8.5 grams.	1000
B.	Æ	27 mm.			7500

Obverse:
Bust of Churchill to right, laurel branch above. Legend: SIR WINSTON CHURCHILL 1874-1965

Reverse:
Churchill's right hand in victory sign. Below: Canadian maple leaf, French fleur-de-lis, American star, and British Union Jack symbolizing the Western allies. Legend: IN WAR-RESOLUTION · IN PEACE—GOOD WILL ·   Left Field: JH (monogram)

Collections:
A.N.S., Ashmolean, Marquess of Bath, Engstrom

51   Atlantic Charter 25th Anniversary Commemorative Medal, 1965

By CAROLINE MAGRATH, United Kingdom

Emitted by English Historical Medals, Ltd., Douglas

Struck by Turner & Simpson Ltd., Birmingham

A.	N	76 mm.	.916	373 grms.	250*

* (numbered)

This piece is a re-issue of the 1941 Atlantic Charter medal emitted by Turner & Simpson. The reverse of the original medal was used as the obverse for this medal, and a wreath type became the reverse for this re-issue. The new issue was to commemorate the 25th anniversary of the important Atlantic Charter.

Obverse:
Profile portraits of Franklin D. Roosevelt and Winston S. Churchill in half-circle medallions, facing, with crossed American and British flags, with olive branch between, connected by a riband with date 1941. Legends under each bust and in central exergue. Legend: TO / COMMEMORATE / THE / ATLANTIC CHARTER   Left Field: ROOSEVELT   Right Field: CHURCHILL

Reverse:
Laurel wreath type, legendless
Collections:
Marquess of Bath

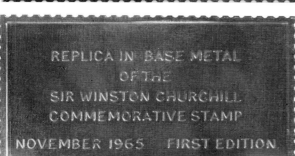

52   Churchill Memorial 1/3 Stamp Plaque, 1965

By MR. and MRS. DAVID GENTLEMAN, United Kingdom

Emitted by the Metalimport Group, London, and Euronummus, Milan

Struck by Johnson, Matthey & Co. Ltd., London
A.   N 41 × 25 mm.   .750   20 grms.   5000*
B.   Æ gilt 41 × 25 mm.   15.5 grms.   100†
* (numbered)   † (trial strikes)

This piece and the following are replicas of the United Kingdom Churchill memorial stamps 1/3 and 4d issued by the General Post Office, London, in July, 1965. Plaques B of both medals were trial strikings. Plaques A are numbered on the reverse. The dies will be turned over to the Post Office Museum, London for this and the following plaque. One thousand of each were issued by Euronummus.

Obverse:
Close-up bust of Churchill facing, slightly to left, after the Karsh photographic portrait of 1941. A vertical line divides the face from the small crowned head of H.M. Queen Elizabeth II to left, turned slightly facing. The denomination appears below: 1/3

Reverse:
Inscription and number. Legend: REPLICA IN 18ct. GOLD / OF THE / SIR WINSTON CHURCHILL / COMMEMORATIVE STAMP / NOVEMBER, 1965 FIRST EDITION (Plaque B begins: REPLICA IN BASE METAL)

Collections:
Marquess of Bath, Engstrom

53   Churchill Memorial Four Pence Stamp Plaque, 1965

By MR. and MRS. DAVID GENTLEMAN, United Kingdom

Emitted by the Metalimport Group, London and Euronummus, Milan

Struck by Johnson, Matthey & Co., Ltd., London
A.   N 41 × 25 mm.   .750   20 grms.   5000*
B.   Æ gilt 41 × 25 mm.   15.5 grms.   100†
* (numbered)   † (trial strikes)

Obverse:
Bust of Churchill facing, slightly to left, after the Karsh photographic portrait of 1941. A vertical line divides the face from the small crowned head of H.M. Queen Elizabeth II to left, turned slightly facing. The denomination appears below: 4d

Reverse:
Inscription and number. Legend: REPLICA IN 18 ct. GOLD / OF THE / SIR WINSTON CHURCHILL / COMMEMORATIVE STAMP / NOVEMBER, 1965 FIRST EDITION (Plaque B begins: REPLICA IN BASE METAL)

Collections:
Marquess of Bath, Engstrom

54   Churchill Memorial Medal, 1965

By JOSEPH I. HAZELDINE, United Kingdom

Emitted by A. Edward Jones Ltd., Birmingham

Struck by A. Edward Jones Ltd., Birmingham
A.   N 57 mm.   .916   137 grms.   500*
B.   R 57 mm.   .925   84 grms.
C.   Æ 57 mm.
* (numbered)

Obverse:
Bust of Churchill facing, slightly to left. Legend: RT. HON. SIR WINSTON CHURCHILL K.G. O.M. C.H. M.P. 1874-1965

Reverse:
Uniface

Collections:
A.N.S., Marquess of Bath, Engstrom

55 Churchill and the Battle of Britain Commemorative Medal, 1965

By ROY BRADSHAW, United Kingdom

Emitted by Bradshaw & Darlington, Birkenhead

Struck by Arthur Fenwick Ltd., Birmingham

A.	Æ 50 mm.	.925	72 grms.	2000*
B.	Æ 32 mm.	.925	47 grms.	3500*
C.	Æ gilt 50 mm.	.925	73 grms.	
D.	Æ gilt 32 mm.	.925	48 grms.	

* (numbered)

The first five hundred of A and B were issued as sets. Medals C and D were also issued as sets.

Obverse:
Bust of Churchill facing, in inner circle, behind in the left field, an airfield and clouds, right field, plane in clouds, ruins of a city below, legend in outer circle. Legend: NEVER · WAS · SO · MUCH · OWED

Reverse:
Aviator's cap with goggles, protecting St. Paul's Cathedral. In left and right fields, flaming ruins of London. Legend in the outer circle. Legend: BY · SO · MANY · TO · SO · FEW — BATTLE OF BRITAIN —

Collections:
Marquess of Bath, Engstrom

56 Churchill Memorial Medal, 1965

By ALESSANDRO COLOMBO and VINCENZO GASPERETTI, Italy

Emitted by Numismatica Italiana, Milan

Struck by Gori & Zucchi, Arezzo

A.	N 65 mm.	.900	105 grms.
B.	N 55 mm.	.900	70 grms.
C.	N 45 mm.	900	35 grms.
D.	N 32 mm.	.900	17.5 grms.
E.	N 28 mm.	.900	10.5 grms.
F.	N 24 mm.	.900	7 grms.
G.	N 20 mm.	.900	3.5 grms.
H.	Æ 65 mm.	.925	(trial strike)
I.	Alum. 32 mm.		(trial strikes)

Obverse:
Bust of Churchill facing, slightly to left, after an eightieth birthday photographic portrait, 1954. Legend: WINSTON CHURCHILL Left Field: 1874 Right Field: 1965 Reeded Edge

Reverse:
Churchill family arms: a shield quartering the arms of Churchill with those of Spencer. The dexter crest is of Churchill and the sinister is of Spencer, with the motto on the scroll: FIEL PERO DESDICHADO (Faithful Though Unfortunate). Legendless

Collections:
A.N.S., Marquess of Bath, Engstrom

57 Churchill and the Battle of Britain Commemorative Medal, 1965

By GEOFFREY HEARN, United Kingdom

Emitted by Geoffrey Hearn, Numismatist, London

Struck by John Pinches (Medallists) Ltd., London

A.	N 38 mm.	.916	39 grms.	100*
B.	Æ 38 mm.	.958	28 grms.	1000

* (numbered)

The emitter and designer of this medal served in the Royal Air Force in the Second World War and wished to commemorate the R.A.F.'s role in the Battle of Britain, and Churchill's leadership.

Obverse:
Bust of Churchill in "siren suit" to right. Legend: WINSTON CHURCHILL K.G.

Reverse:
Air battle between a British Spitfire fighter to left, diving below a German bomber to right, flak explosions around. Legend in center: THEIR / FINEST / HOUR Exergue: 1940

Collections:
A.N.S., Marquess of Bath, Engstrom

58 Churchill Memorial Medal, 1965

By FRITZ JEANNERET, Switzerland

Emitted by Huguenin Medailleurs, Le Locle

Struck by Huguenin Medailleurs, Le Locle

A.	Æ 60 mm.	.925	86 grms.
B.	Æ 60 mm.		

Obverse:
Bust of Churchill facing, slightly to left, after the Karsh photographic portrait of 1941; sculptured technique with roughened field. Exergue: WINSTON S. CHURCHILL (holographic signature, incuse) Right Field: HUGUENIN FJ

Reverse:
Inscriptional type on field of clouds. Legend: 30th NOVEMBER 1874 / SIR WINSTON / CHURCHILL / 24th JANUARY 1965 Exergue: HUGUENIN

Collections:
Marquess of Bath, Engstrom

59   Churchill Memorial Medal, 1965

By FRITZ JEANNERET, Switzerland

Emitted by Huguenin Medailleurs, Le Locle

Struck by Huguenin Medailleurs, Le Locle
A.   Æ 50 mm.   .925   70 grms.
B.   Æ 50 mm.

Obverse:
Bust of Churchill facing, slightly to left, after the Karsh photographic portrait of 1941, sculptured technique, roughened field. Exergue: WINSTON S. CHURCHILL (holographic signature, incuse) Right Field: HUGUENIN FJ

Reverse:
Uniface

Collections:
Marquess of Bath, Engstrom, Kadman, Oslo

60   Churchill Memorial Medal, 1965

By CAROLINE MAGRATH, United Kingdom

Emitted by Turner & Simpson Ltd., Birmingham

Struck by Turner & Simpson Ltd., Birmingham
A.   N 44 mm.   .916   62 grms.
B.   N 44 mm.   .750   54 grms.
C.   N 44 mm.   .375   40 grms.
D.   Æ gilt 44 mm.   .925   37 grms.
E.   Æ 44 mm.   .925   37 grms.
F.   Æ 44 mm.

Obverse:
Bust of Churchill with cigar to left, legend around. The portrait is after the same artist's 1941 Atlantic Charter medal. Legend: 1874 1965

Reverse:
St. George slaying dragon to right, after Pistrucci.

Collections:
Marquess of Bath

61   Churchill Memorial Medal, 1965

By CAROLINE MAGRATH, United Kingdom

Emitted by Turner & Simpson Ltd., Birmingham

Struck by Turner & Simpson Ltd., Birmingham
A.   N 44 mm.   .916   62 grms.
B.   N 38 mm.   .916   37 grms.
C.   N 32 mm.   .916   22 grms.
D.   N 44 mm.   .750   54 grms.
E.   N 38 mm.   .750   31 grms.
F.   N 32 mm.   .750   19 grms.
G.   N 44 mm.   .375   40 grms.
H.   N 38 mm.   .375   23 grms.
I.   N 32 mm.   .375   14 grms.
J.   Æ gilt 44 mm.   .925   37 grms.
K.   Æ gilt 38 mm.   .925   22 grms.
L.   Æ gilt 32 mm.   .925   12 grms.
M.   Æ 44 mm.   .925   37 grms.
N.   Æ 38 mm.   .925   22 grms.
O.   Æ 32 mm.   .925   12 grms.
P.   Æ 44 mm.
Q.   Æ 38 mm.
R.   Æ 32 mm.

The design of this medal differs slightly from the following piece, for it shows a fuller wreath and slightly different placement of the legend. Numbers minted in each metal and size were not recorded for the medals of this artist.

Obverse:
Bust of Churchill with cigar to left, after the Atlantic Charter medal portrait of 1941 by the artist, legend and bust within a laurel wreath. Legend: 1874 1965

Reverse:
Uniface

Collections:
Marquess of Bath

62   Churchill Memorial Medal, 1965

By CAROLINE MAGRATH, United Kingdom

Emitted by Turner & Simpson Ltd., Birmingham

Struck by Turner & Simpson Ltd., Birmingham

A.	A̸ 76 mm.	.916	271 grms.
B.	A̸ 76 mm.	.750	236 grms.
C.	A̸ 76 mm.	.375	171 grms.
D.	Æ gilt 76 mm.	.925	171 grms.
E.	Æ 76 mm.	.925	171 grms.
F.	Æ 76 mm.		

Obverse:
Bust of Churchill with cigar to left, legend and bust within a laurel wreath. The portrait is after the artist's 1941 Atlantic Charter medal. Legend: 1874 1965

Reverse:
Uniface

Collections:
Marquess of Bath

63   Churchill Memorial Medal, 1965

By CAROLINE MAGRATH, United Kingdom

Emitted by Turner & Simpson Ltd., Birmingham

Struck by Turner & Simpson Ltd., Birmingham

A.	A̸ 51 mm.	.916	126 grms.
B.	A̸ 51 mm.	.750	106 grms.
C.	A̸ 51 mm.	.375	76 grms.
D.	Æ gilt 51 mm.	.925	70 grms.
E.	Æ 51 mm.	.925	70 grms.
F.	Æ 51 mm.		

Obverse:
Bust of Churchill with cigar to left, legend below. The portrait is after that by the same artist on the 1941 Atlantic Charter medal. Legend: 1874-1965

Reverse:
Floral design consisting of an English rose, Scottish thistle, Welsh flower (a daffodil) and Irish shamrock and leaves arising from a common stalk from a mound showing new shoots, all within a quatrefoil interrupted by four fleur-de-lis stops. Legendless. (Reverse from a 1953 Coronation medal).

Collections:
Marquess of Bath

64   Churchill Memorial Medal, 1965

Germany

Emitted by Deutsche Numismatik, Frankfurt-on-Main

Struck by the German State Mint, Karlsruhe
A.   A̸ 80 mm.   .986   350 grms.   50*
* (numbered)

Obverse:
Bust of Churchill facing, slightly to left, after the Karsh eightieth birthday photographic portrait of 1954. Legend: SIR WINSTON

CHURCHILL Left Field: 1874 Right Field: 1965

Reverse:
Inscriptional type in laurel wreath. Legend: CUSUS / UT MEMORIA/ VIVAT (Struck as a Lasting Memorial)

Collections:
Marquess of Bath

65   Churchill Memorial Medal, 1966

By ROLF BECK, United States

Emitted by the Chase Commemorative Society, New York City

Struck by the Medallic Art Company, New York City
A.   Æ 39 mm.   .999   30 grms.   1934*
* (numbered)

This medal was the tenth in the society's issues and was only distributed to members.

Obverse:
Bust of Churchill facing, slightly to left, after the Karsh photographic portrait of 1941. Legend: SIR WINSTON S. CHURCHILL Left Field: 1874 / 1965 Reeded edge

Reverse:
Allied military cemetery with grassy foreground, rows of grave-marker crosses, clouds, treeline, British, French and American flags in background. The Churchill quotation used as the legend is here meant to refer to the allied dead. Legend: NEVER . . . WAS SO MUCH OWED BY SO MANY TO SO FEW Exergue: C.C.S.-66

Collections:
A.N.S., Marquess of Bath, Engstrom, Smithsonian Institution

66   Churchill Prime Minister Commemorative Medal, 1966

By GERALD BENNY and STUART DEVLIN, United Kingdom

Emitted by Medallioners Ltd., London

Struck by Johnson, Matthey & Co., Ltd., London
A.   A̸ 44 mm.   .916   54 grms.   1500*
* (numbered)

This medal is the last of six in a series "Prime Ministers of Great Britain". All have a common reverse, the first five hundred were issued in sets with an additional one thousand Churchill pieces issued singly.

Obverse:
Bust of Churchill in "siren suit" to left. Legend: WINSTON CHURCHILL 1874-1965

Reverse:
Portcullis gate, crown above, three segments of chain around. Legend: PRIME MINISTER OF GREAT BRITAIN

Collections:
Marquess of Bath

67 Churchill and the 25th Anniversary of the Atlantic Charter Commemorative Medal, 1966

By MICHAEL RIZZELLO, United Kingdom

Emitted by the Mayfair Gold Medal Centre, London, and Slade, Hampton & Son Ltd., London

Struck by John Pinches (Medallists) Ltd., London and Johnson, Matthey & Co., Ltd., London

A.	Platinum 60 mm.	.999	124 grms.	10*
B.	Platinum 32 mm.	.999	31 grms.	10*
C.	N 60 mm.	.916	124 grms.	150*
D.	N 32 mm.	.916	31 grms.	250*
E.	R 60 mm.	.958	93 grms.	1000*
F.	R 32 mm.	.958	19 grms.	1000*

* (numbered)

The Churchill medal is one of two in a set commemorating the 25th anniversary of the Atlantic Charter. President Franklin D. Roosevelt is depicted on the other medal. The Placentia Bay meeting of August 14, 1941, saw the signing of the important document which would do much to shape the course of the war and the post-war period. Ten sets of A and B were issued, one-hundred ten sets of of C and 100 sets of D. A new issue in 1968 under the original total issue was of forty sets of C and D and 150 sets of D. For the silver medals there were issues of sets with E and F, as well as F alone.

Obverse:
Full-length figure of Churchill seated on ship's deck facing slightly to left, right hand extended to Roosevelt who extends his hand on the other medal. Legend: · WINSTON S. CHURCHILL · AUGUST 9th 1941 Exergue: RIZZELLO / C

Reverse:
Battleship H.M.S. *Prince of Wales* to left in Placentia Bay, Newfoundland. Legend: THE ATLANTIC CHARTER / PLACENTIA BAY MEETING / 25th ANNIVERSARY

Collections:
Marquess of Bath, Engstrom

68 Churchill Memorial Medal, 1965

By JOSEPH I. HAZELDINE, United Kingdom

Emitted by A. Edward Jones Ltd., Birmingham

Struck by A. Edward Jones Ltd., Birmingham

A.	N 32 mm.	.916	32 grms.	2000*

* (numbered)

This medal was issued using the obverse from the previous medal by the artist in 1965, but adding a reverse and reducing the size.

Obverse:
Bust of Churchill facing, slightly to left, after an eightieth birthday photographic portrait. Legend: RT. HON. SIR WINSTON

CHURCHILL K.G. O.M. C.H. M.P. 1874-1965

Reverse:
Inscriptional type. Central legend: OUR AIM / IS / VICTORY
Legend: WE SHALL NEVER SURRENDER

Collections:
Marquess of Bath

69 Churchill and Smuts Commemorative Medal, 1966

By A. TROMP and DAVID MACGREGOR, South Africa

Emitted by Bickels Coins & Medals (Pty.) Ltd., Johannesburg

Struck by Metal Art (Pty.) Ltd., Pretoria West

A.	N 51 mm.	.750	101 grms.	100
B.	R 51 mm.	.925	67 grms.	750
C.	Æ 51 mm.			1750

Sets of A and the first hundred of B and C were issued. The defaced dies were presented to the Africana Museum in Johannesburg. The medal honors the friendship between Churchill and Smuts. They fought against each other in the Boer War, and worked with each other in the two World Wars. Together they laboured to establish the British Commonwealth.

Obverse:
Head of Churchill facing, slightly to left, in inner circle, legend and two laurel branches beside the dates outside. Portrait by A. Tromp. Legend: WINSTON CHURCHILL 1874-1965

Reverse:
Head of Smuts to right, in inner circle, legend and two laurel branches beside the dates outside. Portrait by David MacGregor. Legend: JAN CHRISTIAAN SMUTS 1870-1950

Collections:
A.N.S., Marquess of Bath, Engstrom

70 Churchill and the Dunkirk Evacuation 25th Anniversary Commemorative Medal, 1966

By EDWARD R. GROVE, United States

Emitted by Presidential Art Medals, Inc., Englewood, Ohio

Struck by Medallic Art Co., New York, N.Y.

A.	N 45 mm.	.999	47 grms.	2500*
B.	Æ 45 mm.			

* (numbered)

This medal is the first of the "World War II Medal Series" of thirty pieces to be issued on the 25th anniversaries of important battles, campaigns and events of the war.

Obverse:
Quarter-length of Churchill facing, head slightly to left, after the Karsh photographic portrait of 1941. Left Field: THE RIGHT / HONOURABLE / WINSTON CHURCHILL Right Field: E. R. GROVE / © 1966 PAM

Reverse:
Scene at Dunkirk: evacuation ship at anchor, two troop-filled small boats rowing out to it, airplanes above, smoke and shell explosions in background. Exergue: DUNKIRK / MAY 26 · JUNE 4 / 1940

Collections:
A.N.S., Ashmolean, Marquess of Bath, British Museum, Engstrom, Smithsonian Institution

71 Churchill Memorial Plaque, 1966

By ALESSANDRO COLOMBO, Italy

Emitted by Damiano Colombo & Figli, Milan

Cast by Damiano Colombo & Figli, Milan
A. Æ 140 mm.   uniface casts

This striking portrait shows Churchill as the confident war-time leader of the Commonwealth. The work was displayed at the F.I.D.E.M. exhibition in Paris in 1967.

Obverse:
Bust of Churchill in "siren suit" to left. Legend: WINSTON CHURCHILL Truncation: A. COLOMBO

Reverse:
Uniface

Collections:
Marquess of Bath, Engstrom

72 Churchill Memorial Medal, 1966

By WERNER GUTBROD, South Africa

Emitted by Australian Medallions (Pty.) Ltd., Sydney and Africana Medallions (Pty.) Ltd., Johannesburg

Struck by Matthey Garrett (Pty.) Ltd., Sydney and E. Tiessen (Pty.) Ltd., Johannesburg
A. N 44 mm.   .750   54.5 grms.   2000*
B. Æ 44 mm.   .999   51 grms.   1†

* (numbered)   † (trial strike)

The medal is one from a set of two in commemoration of Churchill and his close friend Sir Robert Menzies, the Australian and Commonwealth statesman. The medals were only issued in sets, one medal portraying each man, but sharing a common reverse. The limit of sets was not fully subscribed in Australia, and two hundred sets were subsequently issued in South Africa. The medals were modelled and the dies prepared in South Africa in 1966, and sent to Australia for striking. The medals struck in South Africa were issued in 1967. The models were presented to the Museum of Applied Arts and Sciences, Sydney.

Obverse:
Bust of Churchill facing, slightly to left. Legend: RT. HON. SIR WINSTON CHURCHILL ·

Reverse:
Crowned shield bearing crossed British and Australian flags. Lion supporter to right, kangaroo supporter to left, and on the scroll below: 1966. Legendless

The reverse is meant to symbolize the unity of the United Kingdom and Australia, and the bonds of friendship fostered by their leaders portrayed on the medals' obverses.

Collections:
Engstrom

73 Churchill and Leaders of World War II Commemorative Medal, 1966

By CARL MERTEN, Australia

Emitted by Australian Coin Associates, Blakehurst, Australia

Struck by S. G. Pitt & Son Pty., Ltd., Blakehurst, Australia
A. Æ 51 mm.   .999   59 grms.   250
B. Æ gilt 51 mm.   53 grms.   100
C. Æ 51 mm.   52 grms.   250

This medal was struck to commemorate the war-time leaders of the Allies, Winston Churchill, Franklin D. Roosevelt and Joseph Stalin as they met at the Teheran Conference of November 28, 1943.

Obverse:
Conjoined busts of the Allied leaders, Churchill, Roosevelt and Stalin, three-quarters to right, after photographs of the Teheran Conference of 1943. Legend: (sprig) LEADERS · OF · WORLD · WAR · II (sprig)

Reverse:
Coat of arms of the emitting association with legend on the scroll and around the design. Legend: · AUSTRALIAN · COIN · ASSOCIATES

Collections:
Marquess of Bath, Engstrom

74 Churchill Memorial Medal, 1967

By GEOFFREY COLLEY, United Kingdom

Emitted by Slade, Hampton & Son Ltd., London

Struck by Johnson Matthey & Co., Ltd., London

A. A′ 65 mm.   .916   115 grms.   500*
B. Æ 65 mm.   .999   87 grms.   500*
C. Æ 65 mm.   500*

* (numbered)

The medals were only issued as full sets containing A, B, and C.

Obverse:
Bust of Churchill facing, slightly to left, after an eightieth birthday photograph, 1954. He appears in the robes of The Most Noble Order of the Garter. Legend: SIR WINSTON CHURCHILL · 1874 · 1965

Reverse:
The Houses of Parliament as they appeared on the 700th anniversary of Parliament in 1965. Legend: MOTHER OF / PARLIAMENTS

Collections:
Marquess of Bath, Engstrom

75 Churchill Memorial Plaque, 1967

By DORA DE PÉDERY-HUNT, Canada

Emitted by Dora de Pédery-Hunt, Toronto

Cast by Industrial Fine Castings, Ltd., Toronto

A. Æ 102 mm. × 90 mm.   8 uniface casts

This quite unique plaque is simple and powerful. It is perhaps the most original approach to conveying a sense of Churchill's greatness and apartness. The artist wrote: "I have been intrigued by Churchill's formidable back, which in my eyes had more character than the faces of most people around us. The photo showed me, more than any of the others taken of him, the solitude and almost loneliness of a great man."

Obverse:
Solitary seated figure of Churchill, as seen from the rear, after a photo taken in the gardens at Chartwell, 1953. Roughened technique for the field and figure. Legend: CHURCHILL Exergue: Hunt '67 (incuse)

Reverse:
Uniface

Collections:
Marquess of Bath, Engstrom

76 Churchill Memorial Medal, 1967

By ARNOLD MACHIN, United Kingdom

Emitted by The Britannia Commemorative Society, Philadelphia, Pa. and The Britannia Commemorative Society Ltd., London

Struck by The Franklin Mint, Yeadon, Pa., Johnson, Matthey & Co., Ltd., London, and John Pinches (Medallists) Ltd., London

A. Platinum 57 mm.   .999   125 grms.   25*
B. A′ 57 mm.   .916   125 grms.   100*
C. Æ 57 mm.   .999   95 grms.   1000*
D. Æ 44 mm.   .999   40 grms.   2204*

* (numbered)

The medal is the fifth in the series issued by the society. Piece D was issued only to members while the other sizes and metals were sold publicly. Medals A, B and C are in matte finish, while D is a proof finish. The Franklin Mint struck 1395 of D for distribution to the society's North American members, the rest were struck by Johnson, Matthey & Co. for other members. John Pinches struck all medals A, B and C.

Obverse:
Bust of Churchill to left. Legend: · SIR WINSTON CHURCHILL · 1874 · · · · 1965 · Truncation: A.M.

Reverse:
Rampant lion to left, holding an upraised sword, behind, a restored St. Paul's Cathedral portrayed phoenix-like arising reborn from fire. Legend: WE SHALL NEVER SURRENDER Right Field: BCS 5 / 1967 (Britannia Commemorative Society, 5th issue, 1967)

Collections:
Marquess of Bath, Engstrom

77 Churchill Memorial Medal, 1967

By M. JAKSIC, Australia

Emitted by the Sydney Coin Club, Sydney

Struck by Amors (Pty.) Ltd., Sydney

A. Æ 39 mm.   .925   40 grms.   250
B. Æ 39 mm.   250

This piece by Miss Jaksic was issued in 1967 on the second anniversary of the Sydney Coin Club which occurred in 1966. The medal memorializes Churchill and commemorates on the reverse the continuing construction of the great Sydney Opera House.

Obverse:
Bust of Churchill, to left, wearing homburg, and with cigar.
Legend: SIR · WINSTON · CHURCHILL 1874-1965

Reverse:
The Sydney Opera House. Legend: SYDNEY COIN CLUB 2ND
ANNIVERSARY Exergue: SYDNEY OPERA HOUSE / 1966

Collections:
Marquess of Bath, Engstrom

Reverse:
St. Mary, Aldermanbury, Church as reconstructed as part of the
Winston Churchill Memorial and Library at Westminster
College, Fulton, Missouri, clouds behind. Shown is the church
and entrance to the lower-level museum. Legend: · WINSTON
CHURCHILL MEMORIAL · FULTON MO.

Collections:
A.N.S., Ashmolean, Marquess of Bath, Engstrom

78   Churchill Memorial Medal, 1967

By CECILE CURTIS, United Kingdom

Emitted by The Metalimport Group, London and Africana
Medallions (Pty.) Ltd., Johannesburg

Struck by Johnson, Matthey & Co., Ltd., London and E. Tiessen
(Pty.) Ltd., Johannesburg

A. Platinum 40 mm.   .999   62 grms.   25*
B. N 40 mm.   .750   38.5 grams.   300

* (numbered)

This Churchill medal is one of two in a medal set memorializing
Churchill and President John F. Kennedy of the United States.
Issued first in platinum sets in the United Kingdom, three
hundred sets were issued in South Africa. The medals have a
common reverse.

Obverse:
Bust of Churchill facing, three-quarters to right. Legend: SIR
WINSTON CHURCHILL 1874-1965 Exergue: C.C.

Reverse:
Crossed British and United States flags. Legend: TO THE FRIEND-
SHIP OF ENGLISH SPEAKING PEOPLES. Exergue: C.C.
The reverse symbolizes the ties between the United Kingdom
and the United States through a common language and history,
and the losses shared by both countries in the deaths of the
leaders portrayed on each medal's obverse.

Collections:
Marquess of Bath

79   Churchill Memorial and Library Commemorative Medal, 1967

By OSCAR F. KLINKE, United States

Emitted by William R. Scott, Jr., Fulton, Missouri

Struck by Bates & Klinke, Inc., Attleboro, Mass.
A. R 29 mm.   .925   12
B. Æ 29 mm.   1700

Obverse:
Bust of Churchill facing, slightly to right, after an eightieth
birthday photographic portrait. Legend: WINSTON CHURCHILL

80   The Churchill Medal for the Art of Communication, 1968

By DORA DE PÉDERY-HUNT, Canada

Emitted by Henry R. Jackman, Esq., Toronto, Ontario

Struck by Canadian Artistic Dies, Inc., Sherbrooke, Quebec
A. N 50 mm.   .999   62 grms.   15
B. R 50 mm.   .999   50
C. Æ 50 mm.   50

This excellent portrait piece was commissioned by Mr. Jackman
from the artist to serve as the award medal for yearly presenta-
tions to be made for accomplishments in public speaking.

Obverse:
Bust of Churchill facing, slightly to left, after the Karsh photo-
graphic portrait of 1941, roughened technique. Legend: THE ·
CHURCHILL · MEDAL · FOR · THE · ART · OF · COMMUNICATION

Reverse:
Inscriptional type, space for engraved name of recipient in
center. Legend: INTER-SCHOOL · COMPETITION DONOR · H.R.
JACKMAN

Collections:
Marquess of Bath, Engstrom

81   Churchill Memorial Medal, 1968

By S. G. M. ADAMS, United Kingdom

Emitted by M. & E. Adams, Jewellery Manufacturers, Leeds

Struck by M. & E. Adams, Jewellery Manufacturers, Leeds
A. Æ 32 mm.   .999   17 grms.   3
B. Copper 32 mm.   3
C. Alum. 32 mm.   3

This obverse die and the following obverse are two further
Churchill portraits by this artist. As with Adams' other medals
these dies were muled with dies of other medals and previous
Churchill pieces. All were produced by direct engraving into
the die by the artist.

Obverse:
Bust of Churchill, three-quarters left, in "siren suit". Legend:
WINSTON S. CHURCHILL

Reverse:
Passant heraldic lion

Collections:
Marquess of Bath, Engstrom

N.B.—The artist muled this obverse die with several other dies
from other medals creating many varieties with the same portrait
obverse die.

81-I

Obverse:
Bust of Churchill, three-quarters left, in "siren suit". Legend:
WINSTON S. CHURCHILL

Reverse:
Britannia seated to left. Legend: BRITANNIA
A. Æ 32 mm.   .999   17 grms.   3
B. Copper 32 mm.   3

Collections:
Marquess of Bath

81-II

Obverse:
Bust of Churchill, three-quarters left, in "siren suit". Legend:
WINSTON S. CHURCHILL

Reverse:
Lion in defiant attitude to left upon a rocky ground. Legend:
GREAT BRITAIN
A. Æ 32 mm.   .999   17 grms.   3
B. Copper 32 mm.   3

Collections:
Marquess of Bath

81-III

Obverse:
Bust of Churchill, three-quarters left, in "siren suit". Legend:
WINSTON S. CHURCHILL

Reverse:
Kirkstall Abbey in Yorkshire. Legend: KIRKSTALL ABBEY
A. Æ 32 mm.   .999   17 grms.   3
B. Copper 32 mm.   3

Collections:
Marquess of Bath

81-IV

Obverse:
Bust of Churchill, three-quarters left, in "siren suit". Legend:
WINSTON S. CHURCHILL

Reverse:
Kangaroo to left, grassy ground, with rock behind. Legend:
AUSTRALIA
A. Æ 32 mm.   .999   17 grms.   3
B. Copper 32 mm.   3

81-V

Obverse:
Bust of Churchill, three-quarters left, in "siren suit". Legend:
WINSTON S. CHURCHILL

Reverse:
Moose head to left. Legend: CANADA
A. Æ 32 mm.   .999   17 grms.   3
B. Copper 32 mm.   3

81-VI

Obverse:
Bust of Churchill, three-quarters left, in "siren suit". Legend:
WINSTON S. CHURCHILL

Reverse:
Design of boar's tusk and bird of paradise. Legend: NEW
GUINEA
A. Æ 32 mm.   .999   17 grms.   3
B. Copper 32 mm.   3

81-IX

Obverse:
Bust of Churchill, three-quarters left, in "siren suit". Legend:
WINSTON S. CHURCHILL

Reverse:
African elephant facing, grassy ground. Legend: SOUTH AFRICA
A. Æ 32 mm.   .999   17 grms.   3
B. Copper 32 mm.   3

81-VII

Obverse:
Bust of Churchill, three-quarters left, in "siren suit". Legend:
WINSTON S. CHURCHILL

Reverse:
Half-nude Maori maiden seated facing on rock. Legend: NEW
ZEALAND
A. Æ 32 mm.   .999   17 grms.   3
B. Copper 32 mm.   3

81-X

Obverse:
Bust of Churchill, three-quarters left, in "siren suit". Legend:
WINSTON S. CHURCHILL

Reverse:
Bust of King Edward VIII to left. Legend: EDWARD · VIII ·
KING · & · EMPEROR
A. Æ 32 mm.   .999   17 grms.   3
B. Copper 32 mm.   3

Collections:
Marquess of Bath

81-VIII

Obverse:
Bust of Churchill, three-quarters left, in "siren suit". Legend:
WINSTON S. CHURCHILL

Reverse:
Facing lion's head. Legend: NIGERIA
A. Æ 32 mm.   .999   17 grms.   1

81-XI

Obverse:
Bust of Churchill, three-quarters left, in "siren suit". Legend:
WINSTON S. CHURCHILL

Reverse:
Bust of H.R.H. the Duke of Windsor, three-quarters left.
Legend: H.R.H. THE DUKE OF WINDSOR
A. Æ 32 mm.   .999   17 grms.   1

82 Churchill Memorial Medal, 1968

By S. G. M. ADAMS, United Kingdom

Emitted by M. & E. Adams, Jewellery Manufacturers, Leeds.

Struck by M. & E. Adams, Jewellery Manufacturers, Leeds
A. Æ 32 mm.   .999   17 grms.   3
B. Copper 32 mm.   3

This portrait followed the preceding medal, and the die was muled with the artist's previous medals. A series of reverse dies commemorating the Commonwealth allies of the war was struck with this obverse and the previous obverse die.

Obverse:
Bust of Churchill, three-quarters right, with bow tie. Legend: WINSTON S. CHURCHILL

Reverse:
Passant heraldic lion to left.

Collections:
Marquess of Bath

N.B.—The artist muled this obverse die with several other dies from other medals creating many varieties with the same portrait obverse die.

82-I

Obverse:
Bust of Churchill, three-quarters right, with bow tie. Legend: WINSTON S. CHURCHILL

Reverse:
Britannia seated to left. Legend: BRITANNIA
A. Æ 32 mm.   .999   17 grms.   3
B. Copper 32 mm.   3
C. Alum. 32 mm.   3

Collections:
Marquess of Bath, Engstrom

82-II

Obverse:
Bust of Churchill, three-quarters right, with bow tie. Legend: WINSTON S. CHURCHILL

Reverse:
Lion in defiant attitude to left upon a rocky ground. Legend: GREAT BRITAIN
A. Æ 32 mm.   .999   17 grms.   3
B. Copper 32 mm.   3

82-III

Obverse:
Bust of Churchill, three-quarters right, with bow tie. Legend: WINSTON S. CHURCHILL

Reverse:
Kirkstall Abbey in Yorkshire. Legend: KIRKSTALL ABBEY
A. Æ 32 mm.   .999   17 grms.   3
B. Copper 32 mm.   3

82-IV

Obverse:
Bust of Churchill, three-quarters right, with bow tie. Legend: WINSTON S. CHURCHILL

Reverse:
Kangaroo to left, grassy ground, with rock behind. Legend: AUSTRALIA
A. Æ 32 mm.   .999   17 grms.   3
B. Copper 32 mm.   3

82-V

Obverse:
Bust of Churchill, three-quarters right, with bow tie. Legend:
WINSTON S. CHURCHILL

Reverse:
Moose head to left. Legend: CANADA
A. Æ 32 mm.   .999   17 grms.   3
B. Copper 32 mm.   3

82-VIII

Obverse:
Bust of Churchill, three-quarters right, with bow tie. Legend:
WINSTON S. CHURCHILL

Reverse:
Facing lion's head. Legend: NIGERIA
A. Æ 32 mm.   .999   17 grms.   1

82-VI

Obverse:
Bust of Churchill, three-quarters right, with bow tie. Legend:
WINSTON S. CHURCHILL

Reverse:
Design of boar's tusk and bird of paradise. Legend: NEW
GUINEA
A. Æ 32 mm.   .999   17 grms.   3
B. Copper 32 mm.   3

82-IX

Obverse:
Bust of Churchill, three-quarters right, with bow tie. Legend:
WINSTON S. CHURCHILL

Reverse:
African elephant facing, grassy ground. Legend: SOUTH AFRICA
A. Æ 32 mm.   .999   17 grms.   3
B. Copper 32 mm.   3

82-VII

Obverse:
Bust of Churchill, three-quarters right, with bow tie. Legend:
WINSTON S. CHURCHILL

Reverse:
Half-nude Maori maiden seated facing on rock. Legend:
NEW ZEALAND
A. Æ 32 mm.   .999   17 grms.   3
B. Copper 32 mm.   3

82-X

Obverse:
Bust of Churchill, three-quarters right, with bow tie. Legend:
WINSTON S. CHURCHILL

Reverse:
Bust of King Edward VIII to left. Legend: EDWARD · VIII ·
KING · & · EMPEROR
A. Æ 32 mm.   .999   17 grms.   3
B. Copper 32 mm.   3
Collections:
Marquess of Bath

82-XI

Obverse:
Bust of Churchill, three-quarters right, with bow tie. Legend:
WINSTON S. CHURCHILL

Reverse:
Uniface. Engraved Legend: SIR W.S. CHURCHILL / 1874-1965.
A.   Æ 32 mm.   .999   17 grms.   3
B.   Copper 32 mm.   3

Collections:
Marquess of Bath

83   Churchill Memorial Medal, 1968

By S. G. M. ADAMS, United Kingdom

Emitted by M. & E. Adams, Jewellery Manufacturers, Leeds
Struck by M. & E. Adams, Jewellery Manufacturers, Leeds
A.   Æ 32 mm.   .999   17 grms.   2

This portrait medal and the following piece were part of the
artist's series of Churchill medals and were meant to fill the
previous void of medals depicting Churchill in formal naval
attire.

Obverse:
Bust of Churchill in naval uniform, three-quarters to right.
Legend: WINSTON S. CHURCHILL

Reverse:
Facing lion's head. Legend: NIGERIA

Collections:
Engstrom

82-XII

Obverse:
Bust of Churchill, three-quarters right, with bow tie. Legend:
WINSTON S. CHURCHILL

Reverse:
Uniface. Engraved Legend: SIR / W.S. CHURCHILL / 1874-1965
A.   Æ 32 mm.   .999   17 grms.   3

Collections:
Marquess of Bath

83-I

Obverse:
Bust of Churchill in naval uniform, three-quarters to right.
Legend: WINSTON S. CHURCHILL

Reverse:
Bust of H.R.H. the Duke of Windsor, three-quarters left.
Legend: H.R.H. THE DUKE OF WINDSOR

A.   Æ 32 mm.   .999   17 grms.   1

82-XIII

Obverse:
Bust of Churchill, three-quarters right, with bow tie. Legend:
WINSTON S. CHURCHILL

Reverse:
Bust of H.R.H. the Duke of Windsor, three-quarters left.
Legend: H.R.H. THE DUKE OF WINDSOR

A.   Æ 32 mm.   .999   17 grms.   1

84   Churchill Memorial Medal, 1968

By S. G. M. ADAMS, United Kingdom

Emitted by M. & E. Adams, Jewellery Manufacturers, Leeds
Struck by M. & E. Adams, Jewellery Manufacturers, Leeds
A.   Æ 32 mm.   .999   17 grms.   2

Obverse:
Bust of Churchill in naval uniform to left. Legend: WINSTON S.
CHURCHILL

Reverse:
Moose head to left. Legend: CANADA

Collections:
Engstrom

84-I

Obverse:
Bust of Churchill in naval uniform to left. Legend: WINSTON S. CHURCHILL

Reverse:
Bust of H.R.H. the Duke of Windsor, three-quarters left. Legend H.R.H. THE DUKE OF WINDSOR
A. Æ 32 mm. .999 17 grms. 1

85 Churchill World War II Leader Commemorative Medal, 1968

By VINCENZO GASPERETTI, Italy

Emitted by Numismatica Italiana, Milan

Struck by Gori and Zucchi, Arezzo
A. N 32 mm. .900 17.5 grms.
B. N 20 mm. .900 3.5 grms.
C. Æ 32 mm. .925 15 grms. (trial strike)

The piece is one of eighteen from a series issued by the firm and its foreign branches on "Leaders in the Second War". The medals share a common reverse of interesting design.

Obverse:
Bust of Churchill facing, slightly to left, after an eightieth birthday photographic portrait. Legend: LEADERS IN THE SECOND WAR 1939 1945 CHURCHILL Upper Field: G.B. (Great Britain) Truncation: VG (monogram)

Reverse:
Legend around an inner circle, the upper part of which shows two arms with swords locked in combat, an atomic bomb mushroom cloud behind symbolizing the war. Below, hands clasped in friendship beneath an arch of eight flags symbolizing the United Nations and the path of post-war co-operation. Legend: POST NUBILA PHOEBUS (After the Clouding the Sun)

Collections:
Marquess of Bath, Engstrom

86 Churchill "Iron Curtain" Speech Memorial Medal, 1969

By FRANK GASPARRO, EDGAR Z. STEEVER and PHILIP E. FOWLER, United States

Emitted by the Fulton Area Chamber of Commerce, Fulton, Missouri

Struck by the United States Mint, Philadelphia, Pennsylvania
A. N 40 mm. .900 1
B. Æ 40 mm. .925 31 grms. 5000
C. Æ 40 mm. 8000

This official U.S. National Medal was struck in commemoration of the dedication of the Winston Churchill Memorial and Library at Westminster College in Fulton. On March 5, 1946, Churchill delivered his portentous "Iron Curtain" speech (actually entitled "Sinews of Peace") at this small college located in the then-President Truman's home state of Missouri, and received an honorary degree.

As a monument to Churchill and his speech, the college's president conceived the idea of reconstructing on his campus Sir Christopher Wren's St. Mary, Aldermanbury, Church. The London church had been badly damaged by bombing in World War II and through the co-operation and interest of many governmental and private individuals the church was shipped stone by stone to Fulton and restored to its full 17th century elegance. The church, with its additional library and museum was dedicated in May, 1969 and for this occasion the local chamber of commerce commissioned a medal which was approved by Congress and struck by the mint. A gold striking was made for presentation to Lady Churchill, and the cancelled dies of this medal were presented to the memorial. By the authorization, silver and bronze medals were struck until December 31, 1969.

Obverse:
Bust of Churchill, three-quarters right, in academical gown and bow tie, after news photographs of the event. Legend: MARCH 5, 1946 · "IRON CURTAIN" SPEECH · FULTON, MISSOURI WESTMINSTER COLLEGE Truncation: FG (Frank Gasparro, Chief Engraver, U.S. Mint) Mintmark: P.

Reverse:
The Winston Churchill Memorial and Library, formerly, the Church of St. Mary, Aldermanbury. Legend: · WINSTON CHURCHILL MEMORIAL AND LIBRARY · WESTMINSTER COLLEGE, FULTON, MISSOURI. Left Field: DEDICATED / MAY 7 / 1969 Exergue: ES, PF (Edgar Z. Steever, mint sculptor, reverse designer, Philip E. Fowler, mint sculptor, modeller of the memorial building)

Collections:
A.N.S., Ashmolean, Marquess of Bath, British Museum, Churchill Memorial and Library, Engstrom

88 Churchill and the 25th Anniversary of Peace in Europe Commemorative Medal, 1970

By DAVID CORNELL, United Kingdom

Emitted by John Pinches (Medallists) Ltd., London

Struck by John Pinches (Medallists) Ltd., London
A.   Platinum 44 mm.   .999   4*
B.   Æ gilt 44 mm.   .999   300*
C.   Æ 44 mm.   .999   42 grms.   250*
D.   Æ 44 mm.   300*
* (numbered)

This medal and medals 89, 90 and 91 were issued as sets of four in each metal, cased and edge numbered.

Obverse:
Quarter-length figure of Churchill, three-quarters to right with right hand raised in victory sign, and smoking cigar after the photograph of Churchill arriving in France to receive the Médaille Militaire from M. Ramadier, Premier of France, in 1947. Legendless. Truncation: CORNELL (incuse)

Reverse:
Inscribed tablet, facing lion head above, British flags on right and left of tablet. Central Legend: NEVER IN / THE FIELD OF / HUMAN CONFLICT / WAS SO MUCH / OWED BY / SO MANY / TO . . SO FEW. (Incuse, from his address on the war situation to the House of Commons, August 20, 1940)

Collections:
Marquess of Bath, Engstrom

89 Churchill and the 25th Anniversary of Peace in Europe Commemorative Medal, 1970

By DAVID CORNELL, United Kingdom

Emitted by John Pinches (Medallists) Ltd., London

Struck by John Pinches (Medallists) Ltd., London
A.   Platinum 44 mm.   .999   4*
B.   Æ gilt 44 mm.   .999   300*
C.   Æ 44 mm.   .999   42 grms.   250*
D.   Æ 44 mm.   300*
* (numbered)

This medal and medals 88, 90 and 91 were issued as sets of four in each metal, cased and edge numbered.

Obverse:
Bust of Churchill to left in military uniform and hat, as a Colonel of the Royal Sussex Regiment from several wartime photographs. Legendless. Truncation: CORNELL (incuse)

87 Churchill and D-Day 25th Anniversary Commemorative Medal, 1969

By OSCAR NEMON, United Kingdom

Emitted by International Numismatic Agency, New York City

Struck by Medallic Art Company, New York City
A.   Æ 64 mm.   .999   2500*
B.   Æ 64 mm.
* (numbered)

This important portrait piece, by the designer of the Churchill Crown, is the artist's definitive medallic portrait of Churchill. Its vital style conveys the same energy as the artist's other Churchill works: the siren-suited bust at Windsor, the statue in the House of Commons, and the commemorative crown. The artist prepared several models before the final model was completed in 1969. The medal was issued in 1970. The first 150 silver specimens are housed in presentation cases with a numbered bronze specimen with matching serial number.

Obverse:
Head of Churchill to right. Legend: CHURCHILL D-DAY 1944 Truncation: NEMON (incuse)

Reverse:
Churchill family arms; a shield quartering the arms of Churchill with those of Spencer. The dexter crest is of Churchill, and the sinister crest is of Spencer. The motto on the scroll is FIEL PERO DESDICHADO (Faithful Though Unfortunate). The Garter appears around the shield.

Collections:
A.N.S., Marquess of Bath, British Museum, Engstrom, Smithsonian Institution

Reverse:
Inscribed tablet, facing lion head above, British flags on right and left of tablet. Central Legend: WE SHALL FIGHT ON / THE BEACHES . . . / WE SHALL FIGHT IN / THE FIELDS AND IN / THE STREETS. / WE SHALL FIGHT IN / THE HILLS: / WE SHALL NEVER / SURRENDER. (Incuse, from his address to the House of Commons on June 4, 1940 on the evacuation at Dunkirk)

Collections:
Marquess of Bath, Engstrom

Reverse:
Inscribed tablet, facing lion head above, British flags on right and left of tablet. Central Legend: AT THIS TIME / I FEEL EN-TITLED / TO CLAIM THE / AID OF ALL AND / I SAY "COME THEN, / LET US GO / FORWARD TOGETHER / WITH OUR / UNITED STRENGTH" (Incuse, from his first address as Prime Minister to the House of Commons, May 13, 1940)

Collections:
Marquess of Bath, Engstrom

90 Churchill and the 25th Anniversary of Peace in Europe Commemorative Medal, 1970

By DAVID CORNELL, United Kingdom

Emitted by John Pinches (Medallists) Ltd., London

Struck by John Pinches (Medallists) Ltd., London

A.	Platinum 44 mm.	.999		4*
B.	Æ gilt 44 mm.	.999	42 grms.	300*
C.	Æ 44 mm.	.999	42 grms.	250*
D.	Æ 44 mm.			300*

* (numbered)

This medal and medals 88, 89, and 91 were issued as sets of four in each metal, cased and edge numbered.

Obverse:
Bust of Churchill to left, facing three-quarters to left, in a pensive mood after photographs taken at the B.B.C. during his "End of the War in Europe" world broadcast May 8, 1945. Legendless. Truncation: CORNELL (incuse)

Reverse:
Inscribed tablet, facing lion head above, British flags on right and left of tablet. Central Legend: IF THE / BRITISH EMPIRE / AND ITS COMMONWEALTH / LAST FOR A / THOUSAND YEARS, / MEN WILL STILL SAY: / "THIS WAS THEIR / FINEST HOUR". (Incuse, from his B.B.C. broadcast "This Was Their Finest Hour" of June 18, 1940)

Collections:
Marquess of Bath, Engstrom

91 Churchill and the 25th Anniversary of Peace in Europe Commemorative Medal, 1970

By DAVID CORNELL, United Kingdom

Emitted by John Pinches (Medallists) Ltd., London

Struck by John Pinches (Medallists) Ltd., London

A.	Platinum 44 mm.	.999		4*
B.	Æ gilt 44 mm.	.999	42 grms.	300*
C.	Æ 44 mm.	.999	42 grms.	250*
D.	Æ 44 mm.			300*

* (numbered)

This and the preceding three medals were issued in sets of four in each metal, cased and edge numbered.

Obverse:
Bust of Churchill, three-quarters to left, in front of microphone after several wartime photographs. Legendless. Truncation: CORNELL (incuse)

PART II *Coins*

92 Churchill Commemorative Crown, 1965

By MARY GILLICK and OSCAR NEMON, United Kingdom

Emitted by the United Kingdom

Struck by the Royal Mint, London

A. Cupro-nickel 39 mm.   28 grms.   19,640,000

The intention to issue a Churchill crown was announced on March 16, 1965. Only four commemorative coins have been issued in the U.K., and this coin is the first with the head of a subject placed on the same coin as that of the monarch, and the first since the Commonwealth to portray a commoner in 1953. The obverse is the design accepted for the new coinage in 1953. The reverse was designed by Oscar Nemon and is in a low relief in a rough sculptured technique. Nemon met Churchill in Marrakesh in 1950 and they became close friends. His portrait for the coin was derived from the Churchill portrait bust Nemon prepared for Her Majesty, The Queen. The siren-suited likeness is now at Windsor Castle.

The following Royal Proclamation was made on August 3rd:

BY THE QUEEN
A PROCLAMATION
DETERMINING THE DESIGN FOR THE CUPRO-NICKEL CROWN PIECE COMMEMORATING THE LATE THE RIGHT HONOURABLE SIR WINSTON LEONARD SPENCER CHURCHILL.

ELIZABETH R.

Whereas under section eleven of the Coinage Act, 1870, We have power, with the advice of Our Privy Council, from time to time by Proclamation to determine the design for any coin:

And Whereas it appears to Us desirable to determine a new design, herein-after specified, for the cupro-nickel Crown, being one of the cupro-nickel coins mentioned in the Schedule to the Coinage Act, 1946, to be struck at Our Mint in London in commemoration of Our Right Trusty and Well-Beloved Counsellor, Sir Winston Leonard Spencer Churchill, Knight of Our Most Noble Order of the Garter, Member of the Order of Merit, Member of the Order of the Companions of Honour, upon whom had been conferred the Territorial Decoration, deceased:

We, therefore, in pursuance of the said section eleven and of all other powers enabling Us in that behalf, do hereby, by and with the advice of Our Privy Council, proclaim, direct and ordain as follows:—

Notwithstanding anything contained in Our Proclamation of the fourth day of October, One thousand nine hundred and

fifty-three, the design for the cupro-nickel Crown to be struck at Our Mint in London in commemoration of the said Sir Winston Leonard Spencer Churchill shall be as follows:—

For the obverse impression Our Effigy with the inscription "ELIZABETH II DEI GRATIA REGINA F.D." and below the date of the year "1965", and for the reverse the effigy of the said Sir Winston Leonard Spencer Churchill with the word "CHURCHILL". The coin shall have a graining upon the edge.

This Proclamation shall come into force on the sixth day of August, One thousand nine hundred and sixty-five.

Given at Our Court at Buckingham Palace, this third day of August, in the year of our Lord One thousand nine hundred and sixty-five, and in the Fourteenth year of Our Reign.

GOD SAVE THE QUEEN

Lady Churchill started the coining press in September, receiving the first Churchill crown. Distribution to the public began on October 11, 1965, and production continued until the summer of 1966 to supply the demand for the coin and its controversial portrait of Sir Winston. The Queen, on a visit to the Royal Mint, coined one of the crowns which was then presented to Lady Churchill.

Obverse:
Head of Her Majesty Queen Elizabeth II to right by Mary Gillick. Legend: ELIZABETH II DEI GRATIA REGINA F.D. 1965 Truncation: M.G.

Reverse:
Bust of Churchill in "siren suit" to right by Oscar Nemon, after the artist's Churchill bust at Windsor Castle. Legend: CHURCHILL

Collections:
A.N.S., Ashmolean, Marquess of Bath, British Museum, Engstrom, Fitzwilliam, Kadman, National Maritime Museum, Oslo, Smithsonian Institution

93 Churchill Commemorative Riyal, 1965

By ROBERT COCHET, France

Emitted by the Mutawakelite Kingdom of Yemen

Struck by the French Mint, Paris

A. Æ 36 mm.   .720   25 grms.   470*
B. Æ 36 mm.   .720   25 grms.   6000
* (essais)

These pieces were coined in Paris in March, 1966, under decree of the Imam al-Badr, commander of the Royal Yemeni forces. As the royalist government was attempting to regain the Yemen from the Republic of Yemen government, there has been some question as to the status of the Churchill riyal as an official coin. The following is an English translation of the official decree for the coin as provided by Brigadier General B. A. de Bourbon-Condé. The decree was in Arabic on paper showing the arms of the Royal Yemen Diwan:

In the Name of God the Merciful, the Beneficent,

We, the Imam al-Mansur Billah Mohammed al-Badr, King of the Mutawakelite Kingdom of Yemen, do authorize our Ministry of Communications, in consideration of the friendship and support for our Cause by the late great world statesman Sir Winston Churchill of Great Britain, and in memory of his great services to world peace and security and to mankind in general in so many fields of endeavour, to strike a memorial coin with the effigy of Sir Winston on the face and our Royal Arms on the reverse, with appropriate commemorative texts and our national superscription, in the value of one silver riyal each, and the appropriate details of design, quantities of ordinary coins and of essais, weight, quality, etc. are to be attended to by our Communications Adviser, Colonel Abdurrahman B. A. de Bourbon-Condé, of our Royal General Staff.

Given at Royal General Headquarters, Camp al-Mansur, Yemen, this —— day of ——— the year 1385, corresponding to ——— 1965.

(signed) Mohammed al-Badr

Obverse:
Bust of Churchill facing, slightly to left, after the Karsh eightieth birthday photographic portrait of 1954. Similar legends appear in both Arabic and English. Legend: · IN MEMORIAM SIR WINSTON CHURCHILL 1965 · Right Field: RC (monogram)

Reverse:
Crowned Royal Yemen arms. Similar legends in both Arabic and English. Left and Right Fields: 720 Winged A (monogram of the French Mint, Paris). Legend: THE MUTAWAKELITE KINGDOM OF YEMEN YEAR 1385 (in Arabic) Exergue: YEMEN (in English) / ONE RIAL (in Arabic and English). ESSAI appears above the Royal Arms on specimens of type A.

Collections:
A.N.S.. Marquess of Bath, Engstrom

Index of Artists
Referenced to Catalogue Entry Number

Artist Unknown 17, 18, 64
Adams, S. G. M. 27, 27-I to 27-IX, 28, 41, 41-I to 41-IX, 81, 81-I to 81-XI, 82, 82-I to 82-XIII, 83, 84, 84-I
Affer, C. 16, 29, 33, 34
Andrechuk, A. 26
Beck, R. 65
Benny, G. 66
Bradshaw, R. 55
Cademartori, R. 19, 25
Casto, M. 36
Cavallo, B. 40
Centeno-Vallenilla, P. 19
Churchill, W. S. 13, 14
Cochet, R. 93
Colley, G. 50, 74
Colombo, A. 56, 71
Cornell, D. 88, 89, 90, 91
Curtis, C. 78
Devlin, S. 66
Diller, H. 43
Eberbach. W. 1
Foley, A. M. 46
Fowler, P. E. 86
Galdini, R. 21
Galoppi, B. 44
Gasparro, F. 86
Gasperetti, V. 56, 85
Gentleman, Mr. & Mrs. D. 52, 53
Gillick, M. 92
Goetz, G. 3, 4, 5
Goetz, K. 2
Grove, E. R. 70
Gutbrod, W. 72
Hahn, Mr. & Mrs. E. 42
Halnon, F. J. 8
Hayman, S. 9
Hazeldine, J. I. 54, 68
Hearn, G. 57
Hotter, J. 49
Hunt, D. de Pédery 75, 80
Hunt, K. C. 46
Ironside, C. 23
Jaksic, M. 77
Jeanneret, F. 58, 59
Klinke, O. F. 79
Kohler, E. J. 37, 38
Kormis, F. I. 6
Kovacs, F. 15, 20, 30, 45
Loewental, A. 12, 35
Lombardo, O. N. 48
MacGregor, D. 69
Machin, A. 76
Magrath, C. 7, 51, 60, 61, 62, 63
Menconi, R. 31
Merten, C. 73
Nemon, O. 87, 92
Pater, W. A. 37, 38
Pédery-Hunt, D. de 75, 80
Pinches, L. E. 39
Rizzello, M. 67
Salomon, H. 32

Schmidt, R. 22
Spicer-Simson, T. 10
Steever, E. Z. 86
Tromp, A. 69
Turin, P. 11
Vincze, P. 47
Vis, W. 24
Wynwood, E. 42

Estimated Valuations

The following valuations are based on issue prices, when followed by asterisk (which includes U.K. purchase tax at issue where applicable) and valuations based on recent auction and dealers' prices. Several medals are unpriced if the medal has not appeared on the market or is especially rare. Valuations are for uncirculated medals, cased and with proper certification if so issued.

Valuations are given in U.K. Pounds and U.S. Dollars at the rate of 1 Pound to $2.60.

Ref	£	$
1A	£10.00	$26.00
2A	£20.00	$52.00
B	£20.00	£52.00
C	£20.00	$52.00
D	£15.00	$39.00
3A	£20.00	$52.00
B	£15.00	$39.00
C	£20.00	$52.00
4A	£20.00	$52.00
B	£15.00	$39.00
5A	£25.00	$65.00
B	£15.00	$39.00
6A	£60.00	$156.00
7A	—	—
8A	£10.00	$26.00
9A	—	—
10A	—	—
B	£50.00	$130.00
11A	—	—
B	—	—
C	£12.00	$31.00
D	£4.00	$10.40
12A	£10.00	$26.00
13A	£100.00	$260.00
14A	—	—
15A	£30.00	$78.00
B	£25.00	$65.00
16A	—	—
17A	£3.00	$7.80
B	£2.00	$5.20
18A	£3.00	$7.80
B	£2.00	$5.20
19A	£15.00	$39.00
B	£7.00	$18.20
C	£3.00	$7.80
D	£2.00	$5.20
20A	—	
B	£50.00	$130.00
21A	£15.00	$39.00
B	£8.00	$20.80
C	£10.00	$26.00
22A	£40.00	$104.00*
B	£15.00	$39.00*
C	£3.00	$7.80*
D	£10.00	$26.00
23A	£125.00	$325.00
B	£30.00	$78.00 } £170.00 $442.00 set*
C	£3.00	$7.80
D	£10.00	$26.00*
E	£10.00	$26.00
24A	£70.00	$182.00*
B	£20.00	$104.00*
C	£15.00	$39.00*
D	£7.00	$18.20*
E	£6.50	$16.90
F	£4.00	$10.40*
G	£10.00	$26.00
H	£6.00	$15.60
I	£5.00	$13.00
J	£4.00	$10.40
K	£3.00	$7.80

Ref	£	$
L	£2.00	$5.20
M	£3.00	$7.80
25A	£16.00	$41.60*
B	£4.00	$10.40
26A	£154.00	$400.00*
B	£10.00	$26.00*
C	£2.00	$5.20
27A	£20.00	$52.00
B	£5.00	$13.00
C	£4.00	$10.40
D	£4.00	$10.40
E	£4.00	$10.40
27-I to 27-IX		
A	£10.00	$26.00
B	£6.00	$15.60
C	£4.00	$10.40
D	£4.00	$10.40
28A	£12.00	$31.20
B	£10.00	$26.00
C	£10.00	$26.00
D	£10.00	$26.00
E	£6.00	$15.60
F	£6.00	$15.60
G	£6.00	$15.60
H	£4.00	$10.40
29A	£15.00	$39.00
B	£14.00	$36.40
C	£9.00	$23.40
D	£4.00	$10.40
E	£8.00	$20.80
30A	£100.00	$260.00* } £150.00 $390.00 set*
B	£35.00	$91.00*
C	£10.00	$26.00
D	£7.00	$18.20
31A	£15.00	$39.00
B	£3.00	$7.80
32A	£50.00	$130.00
33A	£40.00	$104.00
B	£20.00	$52.00 } £90.00 $234.00 set*
C	£15.00	$39.00
D	£5.00	$13.00
E	£30.00	$78.00*
F	£15.00	$39.00* } £60.00 $156.00 set*
G	£9.00	$23.40*
H	£6.00	$15.60*
I	£8.00	$20.80
34A	£65.00	$169.00*
B	£30.00	$78.00*
C	£20.00	$52.00*
D	£10.00	$26.00*
E	£5.00	$13.00*
F	£7.00	$18.20
35A	£105.00	$273.00*
B	£50.00	$130.00*
C	£10.00	$26.00
D	£2.00	$5.20
36A	£6.00	$15.60
B	£1.00	$2.60
C	£1.00	$2.60
37A	£95.00	$247.00*
B	£35.00	$91.00*

Ref	£	$	Notes
C	£5.50	$14.30*	
D	£3.00	$7.80*	
E	£5.00	$13.00*	
F	£2.75	$7.15*	
G	£2.00	$5.20*	
H	£1.00	$2.60*	
38A	£95.00	$247.00*	(A, C, E, G £110.00 $286.00 set*)
B	£35.00	$91.00*	(B, D, F, H £45.00 $117.00 set*)
C	£5.50	$14.30*	
D	£3.00	$7.80*	
E	£5.00	$13.00*	
F	£2.75	$7.15*	
G	£2.00	$5.20*	
H	£1.00	$2.60*	
39A	£420.00	$1092.00*	
B	£175.00	$325.00*	} £600.00 $1530.00 set*
C	£96.00	$249.60*	
D	£45.00	$117.00*	
E	£54.00	$140.40*	
F	£18.00	$46.80	
G	£12.00	$31.20	
H	£7.00	$18.20	
I	£2.50	$6.50*	
J	£1.00	$2.60*	
40A	£6.00	$15.60	
B	£1.10	$2.90	
C	£1.10	$2.90	
41A	£20.00	$52.00	
B	£10.00	$26.00	
C	£6.00	$15.60	
D	£4.00	$10.40	
41-I to 41-VIII			
A	£10.00	$26.00	
B	£6.00	$15.60	
42A	£11.00	$28.60	
B	£10.00	$26.00	
C	£1.50	$3.90	
D	£1.50	$3.90	
43A	£150.00	$390.00*	
B	£120.00	$312.00*	
C	£95.00	$247.00*	
D	£60.00	$156.00*	
E	£30.00	$78.00*	
F	£15.00	$39.00*	
G	£10.00	$26.00*	
H	£4.00	$10.40*	
I	£8.00	$20.80	
44A	£75.00	$195.00	
45A	—	—	} £975.00 $2535.00 set
B	—	—	
C	£110.00	$286.00*	} £160.00 $416.00 set*
D	£40.00	$104.00*	
E	£12.50	$32.50*	
F	£10.00	$26.00	} £12.00 $31.20 set*
G	£6.00	$15.60	
46A	£45.00	$117.00	
B	£8.00	$20.80	
C	£2.00	$5.20	
47A	—	—	
B	£8.00	$20.80	
48A	£15.00	$39.00	
B	£4.00	$10.40	
C	£1.50	$3.90	
D	£1.00	$2.60	
E	£0.25	$0.65	
49A	£3.00	$7.80	
B	£1.00	$2.60	
50A	—	—	
B	—	—	
C	£116.00	$301.60*	} £142.50 $370.50 set*
D	£21.00	$54.60*	
E	£15.00	$39.00	
F	£10.00	$26.00	
G	£8.00	$20.80	
51A	£304.50	$791.70*	
52A	£22.00	$57.20*	(52A, 53A £44.00 $114.40 set*)
B	£8.00	$20.80	
53A	£22.00	$57.20*	(52A, 53A £44.00 $114.40 set*)
B	£8.00	$20.80	
54A	£120.00	$312.00*	
B	£11.00	$28.60	
C	£2.00	$5.60	
55A	£18.00	$46.80*	
B	£10.00	$26.00*	} £34.00 $88.40 set*
C	£18.00	$46.80*	
D	£10.00	$26.00*	} £34.00 $88.40 set*
56A	£90.00	$234.00*	
B	£60.00	$156.00*	
C	£30.00	$78.00*	
D	£15.00	$39.00*	
E	£10.00	$26.00*	
F	£8.00	$20.80	
G	£4.00	$10.40	
H	£15.00	$39.00	
I	£5.00	$13.00	
57A	£70.00	$182.00	
B	£8.00	$20.80	
58A	£15.00	$39.00	
B	£3.00	$7.80	
59A	£11.00	$28.60	
B	£4.00	$7.80	
60A	£60.00	$156.00	
B	£23.00	$59.80	
C	£20.00	$52.00	
D	£8.00	$20.80	
E	£8.00	$20.80	
F	£2.00	$5.60	
61A	£60.00	$156.00	
B	£30.00	$78.00	
C	£20.00	$52.00	
D	£23.00	$59.80	
E	£20.00	$52.00	
F	£15.00	$39.00	
G	£8.00	$20.80	
H	£6.00	$15.60	
I	£4.00	$10.40	
J	£8.00	$20.80	
K	£6.00	$15.60	
L	£4.50	$11.70	
M	£8.00	$20.80	
N	£6.00	$15.60	
O	£4.00	$10.40	
P	£2.00	$5.60	
Q	£1.50	$3.90	
R	£1.00	$2.60	
62A	£200.00	$520.00	
B	£110.00	$286.00	
C	£50.00	$130.00	
D	£25.00	$65.00	
E	£25.00	$65.00	
F	£4.00	$10.40	
63A	£90.00	$247.00	
B	£60.00	$156.00	
C	£20.00	$52.00	
D	£8.00	$20.80	
E	£8.00	$20.80	
F	£2.00	$5.20	
64A	£315.00	$819.00*	
65A	£8.00	$20.80	
66A	£60.00	$156.00*	(£360.00 $936.00 set of six*)
67A	£860.00	$2236.00*	(set of two)
B	£220.00	$572.00*	(set of two)
C	£250.00	$650.00*	(set of two) (C, D set of four £510.00 $1326.00* Slade, Hampton)
D	£65.00	$169.00*	(set of two) (D set of two £105.00 $273.00* Slade, Hampton)
E	£15.00	$39.00*	(set of two) } £35.00 $91.00 set of four*
F	£10.00	$26.00*	(set of two)
68A	£30.00	$78.00*	

69A	£115.00	$299.00*			
B	£10.00	$26.00*	}	£130.00	$340.00 set*
C	£5.00	$13.00*			
70A	£8.00	$20.80*			
B	£1.50	$4.00*			
71A	£60.00	$156.00			
72A	£130.00	$338.00* (set of two)			
B	£20.00	$52.00			
73A	£9.00	$23.40*			
B	£4.00	$10.40*			
C	£3.00	$7.80*			
74A	£170.00	$439.00			
B	£20.00	$52.00	}	£199.00	$518.00 set*
C	£10.00	$26.00			
75A	£60.00	$156.00			
76A	—	—			
B	—	—			
C	£15.00	$39.00			
D	£10.00	$26.00			
77A	£9.00	$23.40			
B	£2.00	$5.20			
78A	—	—			
B	£90.00	$234.00* (set of two)			
79A	£12.00	$31.20			
B	£0.50	$1.30			
80A	—	—			
B	—	—			
C	—	—			
81A	£10.00	$26.00			
B	£6.00	$15.60			
C	£5.00	$13.00			
81-I to 81-X					
A	£10.00	$26.00			
B	£6.00	$15.60			
82A	£10.00	$26.00			
B	£6.00	$15.60			
82-I to 82-XIII					
A	£100.00	$26.00			
B	£6.00	$15.60			
C	£4.00	$10.40			
83A	£12.00	$31.20			
84A	£12.00	$31.20			
84-I					
A	£12.00	$31.20			
85A	£15.00	$39.00*			
B	£5.00	$13.00*			
C	£10.00	$26.00			
86A	—	—			
B	£4.00	$10.40*			
C	£0.75	$1.95*			
87A	£19.25	$50.00*	}	£48.00	$125.00 set
B	£5.00	$17.00*			
88 to 91					
A	—	— (88A, 89A, 90A, 91A set)			
B	£35.00	$91.00 (88B, 89B, 90B, 91B set)			
C	£30.00	$78.00 (88C, 89C, 90C, 91C set)			
D	£10.00	$26.00 (88D, 89D, 90D, 91D set)			
92A	£0.50	$1.30			
93A	£4.00	$10.40			
B	£3.00	$7.80			